"Dealing in the field of Sports Medicine and being an athlete myself, I always look for the extra edge. *How To Compete With Yourself And Win!* is such a tool to achieve that advantage on the field or in the boardroom. This text gives examples of various techniques and explains how to apply them toward one's goals.

By following Dino's explanations and directions, it is much easier to follow a pathway toward individual fulfillment.

Now is the time to get the book and begin the process of reaching your full potential. Not only will you learn something, you will enjoy it as well."

OAK BROOK CHIROPRACTIC CENTER
Philip E. Claussen, D.C.

"For a number of years, I worked alongside Dino in the areas of marketing and sales. His knowledge of these fields is exemplary. "How To Compete With Yourself And Win!" takes the basic elements of motivation and spells them out in a detail and depth I have rarely encountered. Anybody who reads the book will find something of value -- some facet or facets that will help toward greater success in our highly-competitive workplace!"

Thomas N. Nicholson III
Chicago District Manager
MICROS Systems, Inc.

"The author has given me more practical insights into motivation than any other motivational book I have ever read. His writing style is easy to read and understand, and his enthusiasm is evident in every word. I have already applied his principles to my own business responsibilities and they work. I strongly recommend this book to anyone who wants to be better than they thought possible!"

Dean Almquist
Vice President and General Manager
Three Rivers Terminal

"Pavlakos presented a motivational seminar to a group of our people which included most levels of responsibility. He spent time with me to determine exactly what I expected from his seminar. The results exceeded our expectations. His dynamic, in-person presentation, his wide range of knowledge, and his ability to involve the attendees far surpass any seminar I have ever attended. His book encompasses that same vitality and power!"

James P. Paganis
Controller, National Material Company

"I have worked with Dino for over five years now. His energy and enthusiasm for the art of sales is second to none.

During our recent seminar, Dino brought us through the sales maze showing how important it is to hear what the customer needs rather than telling the customer what we have to sell. Five minutes with Dino will get your blood flowing and your emotions rushing.

How To Compete With Yourself And Win by Dino Pavlakos makes a statement of how I try to live my life. I believe that the most important person to compete with is yourself because only you can set the pace for your success. Working with Dino I have seen how he lives his life through this message in all that he does and teaches. What's important in our success is the enjoyment we have while afforded life on this earth."

John M. Seelander, Vice-President
The Plus Group, inc. - Helping Staff America

ABOUT THE AUTHOR ...

Through the years, Dino H. Pavlakos has enjoyed a diversified business career. A highly-motivated individual, he has utilized his talents in the areas of public relations, advertising, direct/dealer marketing, and sales promotion/training. Pavlakos also served as vice president of marketing for a nationwide electronic point-of-sale systems firm headquartered in Chicago, IL.

For a number of years, he was a senior marketing consultant for an electronic cash register firm in Washington, DC. For over a decade, he was CEO of a highly-successful private nursing registry which provided nurses to hospitals, nursing homes, and other facilities. Currently, he is President of his own company, Dino H. Pavlakos & Associates, a full service marketing and consulting firm located in Oak Brook, IL.

The author earned a B.S.C. Degree in Marketing from DePaul University and attended Northwestern University's School of Speech. As a professional writer and speaker, he has scripted and narrated industrial sales films, including two award-winning productions.

Pavlakos has observed people at work in almost every level of accountability and responsibility. He feels strongly -- predicated on real life experiences -- that self-motivation is a key ingredient toward helping individuals achieve greater success in the workplace. He also believes that industrial corporations, retailing enterprises, and service industries can significantly enhance their bottom lines with cost-effective applications of motivation.

HOW TO COMPETE WITH YOURSELF AND WIN!

THE ART OF SELF-MOTIVATION IN THE WORKPLACE

DINO H. PAVLAKOS

DINO H. PAVLAKOS & ASSOCIATES • OAK BROOK

Published by Dino H. Pavlakos & Associates
Copyright © 1995 by Dino H. Pavlakos

The original title of this book was
*How To Achieve Instant Motivation
In The Workplace.*

Inquiries should be addressed to Permission Department,
Dino H. Pavlakos & Associates, 1000 Jorie Blvd., Oak
Brook, IL 60521.

Library of Congress Catalog Card Number: 92-90304

ISBN 0-9633539-0-X

Manufactured in the United States of America.

A Dedication

This book is dedicated to my devoted wife, Jean, and my loyal son, Bob. Their patience, understanding, and support during the two years of work on this book, have constantly served as my inspiration and motivation.

My deepest thanks and appreciation to the marvelous people in those companies with whom I have been directly associated and those companies with whom I have served in a consulting capacity. Their input of thoughts and ideas has contributed greatly to this book.

My heartfelt thanks, also, to those people who comprised my seminars and taught me so much in enhancing my understanding of that word, motivation, and its practical applications in the workplace.

****

CONTENTS

****

CONTENTS

STOP! YOU'RE A SUCCESS!

If fame was the only yardstick for having achieved success, I imagine that very few of us in life would be successful! *Think about it!*

If great financial attainment was the only yardstick for having achieved success, I would think that very few of us in life would be successful! *Think about it!*

Success -- in my way of thinking -- is to achieve what you attempt to achieve, utilizing your talents and abilities to the maximum, and then to move forward.

Success -- in my way of thinking -- is made up of an unending series of levels. When success is achieved on a particular plateau, it is only a temporary step on the way to greater successes. Life is a *series* of successes, not simply *one* success.

There is no one success, in my opinion, that says, "All right, stop in your tracks -- you're successful -- there's nothing more to be achieved. It's over!"

Let's take fame. One of the givens is that fame is fleeting, so once it is achieved, that individual must constantly build on that fame and achieve even greater levels of success while the "iron is hot." Fame is no different than anything in life -- it is competitive!

Let's take prosperity. Great financial attainment is only a level, because the competitive instincts say "more!" So those who have it will drive for even greater financial achievement. Prosperity can be fleeting, too. The key factor is that success is a relative word. For those on the lower levels of accountability and responsibility, even the smallest achievement is significant. It is a mini-success building a bridge to greater successes. For those in the middle or top levels of accountability and responsibility, each achievement is also significant to greater successes!

Success breeds motivation and motivation breeds success. *They are almost inseparable!*

SUCCESS

SUCCESS is based on a strong self-esteem, a powerful confidence level, a continual refinement of skills, and an *overpowering desire* to accomplish.

SUCCESS is not the *comparison* of yourself to the gigantic accomplishments of others. Those accomplishments are better utilized to serve as your *inspiration.*

SUCCESS does not happen overnight. Rather, it is the accumulation of many small, *but significant* plateaus of achievement.

SUCCESS can only come from having set a goal to be achieved. When there is no goal, there is *nothing* to achieve.

SUCCESS is but a perspective and can be fleeting. The secret to *continued* successes and *greater* successes is its *maintenance* and *enhancement.*

SUCCESS is neverending in its quest. It should serve merely as a stepping stone to *greater successes.*

SUCCESS is like a *work of art.* When viewed by a variety of people, it encompasses many different dimensions.

SUCCESS is not necessarily tied in to *who* you know. Rather, it is more deeply related to how well you know *yourself.*

SUCCESS is foremost, a *legitimacy of goals and objectives.*

SUCCESS is not to be flaunted at any level. Rather, it is to be treasured for its moment, nurtured, maintained, worked upon, and refined. The flaunting of success on others is elastic at best and can *quickly snap back at you.*

SUCCESS that breeds complacency is the very caveat of SUCCESS.

THE MOTIVATION FOR A BOOK
ON MOTIVATION-

Motivation has always been an important part of my life in the business world. I have seen its positive, beneficial effects on people. Conversely, I have also seen how the lack of it can cause obstacles to success.

For many years, I have looked in the mirror and promised myself that I would someday write a book on motivation. However, when I sat down to put pen to paper, something always came up to change my plans.

*What **didn't** change, however, was the need for motivation in the business world. In my dealings with a variety of people every day in my business career, it became obvious that some individuals were standing still, fearful of moving ahead, lacking confidence and possessing a low self-esteem.*

*Yet I noted that armed with a realization of **what** was holding them back and **why** they were failing to move forward, success could be achieved. In my mind, the framework had to be the ability to be **honest with self,** i.e., an honest self-appraisal. Then and only then could posi-*

tive steps be initiated.

The ability of an individual to motivate himself or herself is within us all, but it has to be carefully extracted, based upon a knowledge of motivational factors.

Understanding motivation requires a comprehension of what self-esteem comprises, what earned self-esteem is all about, what differences exist between lack and loss of confidence, why the "I Can't" factor can be harmful, and so forth.

Motivation is a valuable tool that can be with you for the rest of your life, helping you every step of the way to success.

As you can see, I did find time to write this book for only one reason. **I was motivated to do it!**

A PERSONAL PERSPECTIVE

You see it in action all the time -- this word called *motivation.* It is readily *visible* as a gleam in the eye of the individual who has made a commitment to succeed. You can *hear* motivation in the enthusiastic words of an individual who takes pride in achievement. And you can readily *sense* motivation in an individual who is dedicated to superior performance. Through- out the years, controversy has permeated motivation in the world of business. Why? **Simply because each person is motivated dif- ferently.** Then what are the motivational tools that work? Perhaps they are tangible awards; perhaps they are those extra perks; perhaps they are monetary, ad infinitum. Far be it for me to judge which works best.

However, I do know one thing for sure. Any of the above tools are *after the fact!* What really comes first -- and *must come first* -- is the motivation of *self.* It's no simple task. Since time immemorial, people have *talked* motiva- tion. Few, however, have communicated moti- vation in simple terms, thereby making its almost mystical qualities available to all.

How do you motivate yourself? Do you ask a family member to help you? Perhaps. Do you ask a relative for help? Perhaps. Do you ask a friend to motivate you? Perhaps. What are the secret ingredients that so many seek to discover, yet fall short by the wayside time after time? Is there a clear-cut way to motivation that is unequivocal and unfailing in formula and application? *One would be hard-pressed to find it.*

Yet, there is an approach that can work wonders for you and help you achieve more than you ever thought possible -- one that can serve as your personal foundation for success. But it takes discipline, courage, and confidence -- all neatly wrapped up in one word, *self.*

On the following pages, you will follow one man's opinion of what works. Take it for what it is. But if you faithfully apply its thoughts and pragmatic ideas, you may be pleasantly surprised that what was once dormant in you can erupt into a new, driving force to be reckoned with. But even more than that, you will suddenly find a new *you,* a dynamic individual that can suddenly achieve where achievement was previously thought to be impossible!

You are most welcome to the motivational tools that have worked for me and I have seen work for others -- even in adverse circumstances. By the time you finish this book, there's a strong possibility that you will be able to motivate yourself in *less than 30-seconds!*

And if that leads you to greater heights in this marvelous world of business, this book may rank as one of the greatest investments you have ever made, because the *returns will be dividends in yourself. That would be my greatest wish.*

There's something in this book for everyone -- the top executive, middle manager, supervisor, sales manager, new or veteran salesperson, secretary, office person, retailer, entrepreneur, and other in areas of responsibility too numerous to mention. In essence, I am talking about anyone in the world of business -- regardless of the level of accountability and responsibility -- who wants to be **THE BEST OF THE BEST!**

AN AWAKENING

As a young salesperson for an office products firm, I was doing what many salespeople do -- up-and-down-the-street cold canvassing -- a task which even the hard-nosed professionals can detest. In my situation, this meant calling on retail stores and offices, one after the other. If there has ever been a breeding ground for self-discipline, up-and-down-the-street prospecting fits the bill!

Sure, I could have plunked myself down on a seat in a restaurant at 8:00 A.M., downing four or five cups of coffee, spanning two hours. Then I could canvass for one hour and decide it was lunchtime at 11:00 A.M. Fortunately, that wasn't my style.

For one solid week I had canvassed this particular suburb, peddling my wares in the *best way I knew how*. However, I had failed to raise any viable prospects -- even suspects -- and was at my wit's end. One morning, as usual, I was carrying my compact, case-enclosed adding machine. I was feeling sorry for myself. It seemed as if the business world had conspired to knock me down to a level I had never experienced. In essence, I was in a serious state of *self-pity*.

Suddenly, I heard a commotion from across

the street and turned to see what was happening. It was a neighborhood restaurant with its doors held open and entering it was a man without legs, in a wheelchair. As memory goes, it is impossible to forget the four words he said as he made his entry.

"Good morning, how's everybody?"

I stood there transfixed, amazed and impressed that he was *more concerned about others* than about himself. I thought to myself, "Here's a man with no legs. Shouldn't he be carrying a grudge against the world? Why should *he* care how *anybody else* feels?"

What happened next is indelibly stamped in my memory. I have told and retold this story in one-on-one and group situations. I have seen the reaction of the listener(s) - the hardnosed ones and all - and have marveled at the touching impact. It is motivation at its best - not planned, but something that simply happened.

It was as if a mirror unexpectedly appeared in front of me, right there on that street. I looked into that mirror and was repulsed by what I saw. I was feeling sorry for myself because things weren't going right for me. I was not only *sorry*, but I was a *sorry sight.*

I had absolutely lost confidence in myself. The mirror seemed to disappear and my focus was again on that restaurant. There was laughter and joviality there brought about by a man with no legs. Then what the heck did *I* have to complain about?

The mirror reappeared and I looked at myself again. The same face was there, except it was a face transformed into a *let's go up and down that street and get 'em!* No more self pity! No more feeling sorry for myself! No more *the world's against me!* I picked up my adding machine and since then, I can rarely remember a time that I canvassed with a greater air of enthusiasm and confidence. Sales were the direct result. I can only hope that someday you can experience that same feeling - the adrenaline flowing, confidence and desire at their peaks!

Those days I was a young neophyte salesperson and probably failed to realize why that man without legs had turned me around. I realized as time went on that what had basically happened could be explained in five words: **I was ashamed of myself.**

I also realized another very critical factor: I was ashamed of myself because *I had lost confidence in myself.* It taught me a very valuable lesson in life. **You can only lose confidence** when you're giving your best effort -- striving to achieve -- dreaming those marvelous dreams of doing the impossible. If you have given **less than your best,** and you **think** you have lost confidence, forget it! **You never had any confidence in yourself in the first place!**

In a retrospective of that incident, what really impressed me was *how quickly* my negative *feel sorry for myself* syndrome was transformed into a powerful burst of positive attitude and confidence.

It was like a light switch. One moment I was *off* and then, with the simple *click* of a meaningful event, I was *on!*

There's a valuable lesson to be learned here. When you are truly trying to be the best of the best and you are beset with a lack of confidence, it is only temporary. The key factor is to avoid letting that loss of confidence take you on a prolonged negative path that can *seriously impact your self-esteem and your productivity!*

"WHEN YOU ARE TRULY TRYING TO BE THE BEST OF THE BEST AND YOU ARE HIT BY A LACK OF CONFIDENCE, IT IS ONLY TEMPORARY AND MUST BE TREATED AS SUCH. THE KEY FACTOR IS TO AVOID LETTING A LOSS OF CONFIDENCE TAKE YOU ON A PROLONGED NEGATIVE PATH THAT CAN SERIOUSLY IMPACT YOUR SELF-ESTEEM AND PRODUCTIVITY!"

NEGATIVITIS AND POSITIVITIS

When you are giving that second effort, there is absolutely no reason to be embarrassed when you lose confidence. What is *unnatural* is to let loss of confidence develop into **negativitis.**

Curing negativitis brought about by loss of confidence is treatable with a therapy known as *positivitis.* This means a positive attitude, *self-inflicted.* To make it perfectly clear, if you had a goal, an objective, and a dream that you were going for, the setback to achievement from loss of confidence is only as temporary as you want it to be. **The goal is still there. You are, too. And so are the tools to achieve it.**

Let me make one point at this stage. Occasionally, as you read this book, you may take exception to what is stated, by saying, "This is plain nonsense. It's trite and untrue." But I can assure you that when you finish this book, you'll be convinced that *it's tried and true!*

Back to confidence. Once you recognize that a loss of confidence -- believe it or not -- can be a springboard to greater achievements, to a realization of goals, to fruition of basic objectives, you are thinking correctly. I cannot overemphasize that I am referring to a loss of confidence that comes *only* from a strong effort to be *the best of the best!*

Let's outline procedures that may help you handle loss of confidence, and then we'll discuss each one of them. Throughout this book, you'll find ways and means to *develop* self-confidence.

"CURING NEGATIVITIS BROUGHT ABOUT BY A LOSS OF CONFIDENCE IS TREATABLE WITH A THERAPY KNOWN AS *POSITIVITIS*. THIS MEANS A POSITIVE ATTITUDE, *SELF-INFLICT-ED.*"

HOW TO HANDLE LOSS OF CONFIDENCE

1. The first thing to do is accept it.

2. Treat it as something that occasionally happens when a person strives hard.

3. Attack it immediately.

4. Refuse to be intimidated.

5. Eliminate any negative reaction at once.

6. Access any positive factors from your loss of confidence.

7. Stop the *"everybody's against me"* syndrome in its tracks.

8. Renew your enthusiasm and go for it!

The first thing to do is to accept it. Take it on face value. At this point, don't try to read something into it that is not there. It happened.

Treat it as something that occasionally happens when a person strives hard. Without a doubt, this is really the heart of honesty to yourself. When a person tries to kid oneself that he or she is really trying and really is not, who is *really* being fooled? **That person, that's who!** There are important factors for you to analyze here. For example:

-Were you really trying hard when the lack of confidence occurred?

-Had you perhaps let down your efforts just before you lost confidence?

-How serious were you about achieving? Had you set a goal or an objective?

-Were you honestly using every tool at your command?

-Somewhere along the way, had you taken the time to analyze your strengths and weaknesses and act accordingly?

Think **honestly**; are you really true to yourself? Remember, **a lack of integrity to yourself is self-destructive.**

Attack it immediately. It is critical to accept a loss of confidence immediately, rather than letting it overpower your reasoning. Your first instinct, as mentioned above, should be to accept it. That's a form of healthy attack, because unless you do accept it, you will be in no position to rationalize what follows. The second wave of your attack is to determine if you were trying hard enough. *This self-analysis sets the stage for you to determine* **reasons,** *rather than* **excuses,** *for your confidence loss.*

Always think in terms of *reasons,* rather than *excuses.* **Reasons** are typically looked upon as facts, while **excuses** are subject to doubt. For example, you often hear the phrase, "All you seem to give me are *excuses."* On the other hand, how often do you hear somebody say, "All you seem to give me are *reasons."*

This thought brings up some very interesting points. For example, in my own company, I permit only reasons, not excuses. If somebody tells me that their car broke down on the way to work, and *it is true,* then it is a reason, not an excuse. Let's say something goes wrong with one of our projects, and the reason it has gone wrong is because one of our suppliers failed to follow through on a commitment.

Who faces the music? The supplier? With me, yes, but not with the customer. I cannot give excuses. The *reason* was my supplier. But the client's trust was in *me.* I must answer to the client that it was my fault and then develop alternatives which I can present to the client. If the client feels strongly enough at this point to tell me to forget the project, I am obligated to do so and make whatever amends to that point that are required.

There's a saying I have heard throughout my career which may be very appropriate here. Simply stated, *"Excuses are weak in the face of others' positive actions!"*

Refuse to be intimidated. Whatever you do, don't let *panic* set in! By rendering the reasoning process virtually inoperative, *panic* clouds your mind to reality. The longer you let panic overcome your logic, the longer it will take you to do battle with confidence loss. Remember, you lost confidence, so accept it! Then, analyze the *reasons,* make whatever adjustments are called for, harness the power of **positivitis,** and rebound!

Eliminate any negative reaction immediately.
Obviously, this is easier said than done.
The question we must now ask ourselves is,
"Can it be done?" Well, it probably can, if you
are prepared for it. Without preparation, your
first response to loss of confidence will be one
of shock that it could happen to you. The
second could be one of extreme upset and
disappointment with yourself.

However, what you want to note here is that
the first thing you should be concerned about
is that you remain calm and try to analyze the
reasons that brought on your confidence loss.

As an example, it might be something that
has to do with your **attitude.** Look around.
Perhaps it is a negative attitude stemming from
problems at home or in your working environment.

Remember, the natural tendency of a
person to whom you are speaking or calling
upon is to reject a person with an attitude
problem. It appears to me that the only way to
get back on the right track and regain your
confidence is to face the existing problem head-
on and do what you can to alleviate or eliminate it. Then -- *and only then* -- will you be able
to go about your business.

You *can* elect to go on as you are with the
encumbrance, but in the long run, nothing of

any consequence will be gained. Keep in mind that the faster you can regain confidence, the faster you will be out in the fascinating business world, fighting the battles toward success.

Many of us in our daily lives think that certain problems happen only to us and to nobody else. During my years in the field of sales, sales promotion, sales management, and consulting, I would be hard-pressed to remember one individual who at some point or other in his or her career failed to lose confidence. In anybody's quest to achieve and be the best of the best, it is natural to run into a temporary setback or two. **How it is handled is one of the keys to success or failure.**

Here are some other scenarios which may help you to understand how to access positive factors from loss of confidence:

"Let's face it. I blew it, but by so doing, I'll pay particular attention to that step the next time, and I'll be better for it."

"All right, I was trying **too hard, overreaching,** *looking for the fifth floor where there was no foundation in the first place. I'm thankful for the lesson. Now, I'll take it step by step!"*

"I failed to take advantage of the opportunities that were there staring me in the face, but that's part of a learning experience. Come on, world. I'm ready for you!"

"I lost my temper when I should have remained calm, cool, and collected. And, in retrospect, I should have appreciated the **constructive criticism** *that was aimed at helping me. From now on, I'll be more receptive."*

"Am I the only one that people seem to pick on? Do I really have more troubles than anybody else? Or am I simply feeling sorry for myself? Maybe I am. I'm going to try some positivitis and think about problems as nothing more than **opportunities in work clothes.***"*

A critical self-appraisal will help immensely. You'll be surprised, looking back on the period that set up your loss of confidence, that you will place those situations in perspective as well as the reasons why they happened. Now, you will be able to access positive factors that will help you be better than you ever thought possible! Always bear in mind that the proper treatment for loss of confidence forces an *automatic evaluation* of internal and external factors which led to your negative situation.

Stop the "Everybody's against me" syndrome in its tracks. When you believe that everybody is against you, you are setting up an artificial defense mechanism in your mind which is an impenetrable shield or wall. This undesirable mechanism automatically prevents anything of a positive or constructive nature from entering. You have set in motion the *self-pity* effect which can only grow worse if not attacked quickly. However, once you are able to rationalize what the *real* problem is, your mind will open and the path toward your success will, too.

Renew your enthusiasm, push all negativitis aside, and go for it!

Let me just reemphasize what I stated before, and this must be the background when you face an occasional loss of confidence:

You can only lose confidence when you're giving your best effort – striving to achieve – dreaming those marvelous dreams of doing the impossible. When you have given less than your best, and you think you have lost confidence, forget it! You never had any confidence in the first place!

"YOU CAN ONLY LOSE CONFIDENCE WHEN YOU ARE GIVING YOUR BEST EFFORT -- STRIVING TO ACHIEVE -- DREAMING THOSE MARVELOUS DREAMS OF DOING THE IMPOSSIBLE. WHEN YOU HAVE GIVEN LESS THAN YOUR BEST, AND YOU THINK YOU HAVE LOST CONFIDENCE, FORGET IT! YOU NEVER HAD ANY CONFIDENCE IN THE FIRST PLACE!"

THE CONTAGIOUS MAGIC OF ENTHUSIASM

Whatever your niche in the world of business, enthusiasm is an important element to success.

Enthusiasm is personal power.

Enthusiasm is a strong link in communication.

Enthusiasm generates confidence in many different modes, e.g.,

on the telephone
in one-on-one situations
in interpersonal work environments
in sales presentations
in business relationships
in management discussions
in management presentations
in business presentations, in general
in all areas of retailing
in employee relationships
in customer relationships
in all aspects of business and personal life,
    too numerous to mention.

Enthusiasm is contagious!

Most importantly of all, genuine enthusiasm comes from a strong, *sincere* belief in *self;* a strong, *sincere* belief in *what you do;* and a strong, *sincere* belief in *your talents and abilities.* The people with whom you associate on a daily basis can relate and respond in a positive way. Therefore, it is essential that you make every concerted effort to associate with enthusiastic people.

Realistically, of course, this may not be possible. However, despite the circumstances, permit nothing to hinder your own enthusiasm. In fact, by retaining it, it may rub off on somebody who really needs it. You'll be a better person for it and a greater success for it!

It's no different than a blade of grass that desires to associate with other blades of grass, not weeds!

Phony enthusiasm is offensive to the recipient. I'm sure that in your business or personal life, you have seen the pseudo smiles, the insincere handshakes, the "you're right" agreeable types. These are the types of individuals in whom you will have difficulty placing your trust.

In the real world, a sincere contagiousness can work to your benefit. Be comforted in the fact that I am not speaking of the back slapper, glad-handing, loud type. I'm speaking of someone who is *sincerely* enthusiastic in his or her desire to achieve, and therefore has armed himself or herself with the necessary tools to do a good job.

Although I mentioned those tools before, let's look at them again because of their importance: **a strong, sincere belief in self; a strong, sincere belief in what you do; and a strong, sincere belief in your talents and abilities.**

Genuine enthusiasm not only enhances your confidence level (provided all other factors mentioned are in place), but helps the person(s) listening to you to develop a sense of trust and confidence in you.

Some people may take exception to the preceding statement, countering, "But there is no element of trust in business, anyway." I say *nonsense!*

A corporation built upon integrity does not yield to deceptive or devious practices. In fact, this type of company demands *trust* as the first essential in its dealings with other companies and their representatives. For example, the true professional salesperson has a primary task of setting the *CZ* factor with the prospect -- the Comfort Zone. The CZ will bring about trust and confidence in the salesperson by the prospect. As a result, the prospect is more apt to relate his needs. This will help the salesperson target those needs effectively with his product or service. So attitude -- the **right attitude** -- is essential in every aspect of business.

A few years ago, I was given an assignment to crystallize the entire business philosophy of a middle-sized firm in preparation for an expensive, expansive brochure. Believe it or not, it took me one month! The chairman of the board and the company president would settle for nothing less than what they felt best communicated the message they wanted to say, wrapped up in one word, **trust.**

The final text comprised only five short sentences in paragraph form to accomplish the task. The last paragraph became the company's slogan and is a vivid testimonial to the fact that most companies value trust and integrity.

Our Company's *integrity* is reflected in a rigid adherence to the principles of ethics, honesty and legality.

Our *character* is reflected in a dedicated family of employees.

Our *personality* is reflected in a sincere concern for our customers.

This unique blending makes (company name) more successful.

We care. That's our commitment to you.

"ATTITUDE -- THE *RIGHT ATTITUDE* -- IS ESSENTIAL IN EVERY ASPECT OF BUSINESS LIFE!"

THE ULTIMATE SUCCESS STORIES

Over the years, you and I, as everybody else, have heard soul-stirring stories of men and women who went from the proverbial "rags to riches." And rightfully so. These stories have and will continue to serve their proper function as a means to inspire by example. In many instances, I can personally say that they have had a positive, dramatic impact on me and will continue to do so.

Yet -- and you may disagree with me -- they may also have a *downside effect* on people. In other words, these stories can result in a negative impact for many.

Let me make myself clear. I am a firm believer that in business life, we are in a competitive situation on a daily basis. That's how it should be and that's how the business world operates. **When competition is at the forefront, the business environment gains and the individual gains.** Competition demands performance. Competition demands knowledge. Competition demands creativity. Competition demands a rigid discipline that asks for the **best of the best** approach in everything we do.

But let's face reality! Each individual has his or her own talents and abilities, and the idea is that we use those talents and abilities to their maximum in our quest for success!

Our thesis, however, says that some will achieve more than others and some *will reach the pinnacles of success.* If this is the case, then realism tells us that not everybody will reach those pinnacles -- yet he or she will be contributing to the betterment of themselves, their families, and their companies.

When a person is saturated with the "rags to riches" scenario, he or she is wont to take a realistic, honest evaluation of himself or herself and, in so doing, might say, "I don't have a chance in the world to get to those pinnacles!" What happens next can be self-destructive if he or she says, "*So why should I even try in the first place?*" Those who truly understand their limitations, but have carved out a niche for themselves, will probably be unaffected.

But let's face it. There are others who are absolutely affected by the "rags to riches" syndrome. After having analyzed themselves and surmised that they cannot reach those pinnacles, they feel as if they have let themselves and those around them down and will begin to wonder if anything is worth trying.

Since the individual sets the mind in that particular mode, the thought of trying *anything* is a laborious thought because it is subservient to the pinnacles. However, on the upside, once that individual realizes that he or she *is* something in this world, that he or she can achieve success to *the best of his or her own capabilities,* there is an excellent chance for success. In other words, these same individuals **can achieve realistic goals,** but these goals are dwarfed by the immensity of the aforementioned super achievers.

This is one reason I purposely chose to avoid the super-success stories as a motivational tool in this book, because I think that everyone should realize that individual success is relative and is dependent on **each individual's** talents and capabilities.

So relax. Set goals for yourself that are realistic. Reach those goals and then set further goals that are realistic. Along the way, take advantage of every opportunity offered or that you make. You may find yourself going from springboard to springboard and even surpassing your goals. That's the beginning of success. Plan your work and work your plan. Who knows? **Maybe someday they'll be writing stories about you!**

"SET GOALS FOR YOURSELF THAT ARE REALISTIC. REACH THOSE GOALS AND THEN SET FURTHER GOALS THAT ARE REALISTIC. ALONG THE WAY, TAKE ADVANTAGE OF EVERY OPPORTUNITY OFFERED OR THAT YOU MAKE. YOU MAY FIND YOURSELF GOING FROM SPRINGBOARD TO SPRING-BOARD AND EVEN SURPASSING YOUR GOALS. THAT'S THE BEGINNING OF SUC-CESS. PLAN YOUR WORK AND WORK YOUR PLAN. WHO KNOWS? MAYBE SOMEDAY *THEY'LL BE WRITING STORIES ABOUT YOU!*"

POSITIVE ATTITUDE: SICK OF HEARING THESE TWO WORDS?

Are you the type that takes offense when somebody mentions the words, **POSITIVE ATTITUDE?**

Think about your answer very carefully because your response may give you a valuable insight as to your own basic feelings toward life and opportunities in general.

Before answering, you may want to ask yourself the following questions.

1. Am I sick and tired of hearing POSITIVE ATTITUDE because my situation precludes it?

2. Am I jealous of those who have a POSITIVE ATTITUDE simply because they have it?

3. Am I envious of those who have a POSITIVE ATTITUDE because those who have it are generally achievers?

4. Am I supposed to believe that POSITIVE ATTITUDE can change my destiny?

5. Do I believe that the words POSITIVE ATTITUDE are nothing more than corn?

6. Aren't the words POSITIVE ATTITUDE typically set aside for salespeople only?

7. Isn't POSITIVE ATTITUDE just as trite as "When the going gets tough, the tough get going?" or "Plan your work, work your plan?"

Let's look at some possible answers to these questions:

1. <u>Am I sick and tired of hearing POSITIVE ATTITUDE, because my situation precludes it?</u>

Well, look at your situation closely, whatever it is, and then take another look. You're probably sick and tired of hearing POSITIVE ATTITUDE because you may have dug yourself into **negativitis.** Whether the negativitis is caused by self-pity or a truly bad situation, you have chosen to give up the battle. You have chosen the path of least resistance. You have knowingly convinced yourself that there are no alternatives available to you to turn the tables around.

You have made a personal, unequivocal (or at least you think so) decision to give up and let your situation control and get the best of you. You are now working harder than you have ever worked at anything before in your life to drag yourself down, to be with those who have reached the depths of negativitis. But there is a business world out there into which you probably fit. Give it a try!

2. <u>Am I jealous of those who have a POSITIVE ATTITUDE, simply because they have it?</u>

Let's face it! So many of us might be envious of something somebody else has that we do not possess. But we're not talking here about luxury cars or large homes. We're merely speaking of one particular possession, POSITIVE ATTITUDE. Now it's understandable that it takes hard work and plenty of money to afford the luxury cars or large homes. But what does it cost to hook on to a Positive Attitude? Nothing. **Absolutely nothing!**

3. <u>Am I jealous of those who have a POSITIVE ATTITUDE, because those who have it are generally achievers?</u>

Don't knock it if you haven't tried it! Try following the leaders, by developing your own POSITIVE ATTITUDE. It can't hurt you and will certainly help you. And you needn't ask anybody else as to how to develop a positive attitude. Hopefully this book will help you develop a POSITIVE ATTITUDE.

4. <u>Do</u> <u>I</u> <u>take</u> <u>these</u> <u>words</u> <u>to</u> <u>mean</u> <u>that</u>
<u>POSITIVE</u> <u>ATTITUDE</u> <u>can</u> <u>change</u> <u>my</u> <u>destiny?</u>

That's exactly what you take those words to mean! Just take a look in the mirror and ask these questions, just to name a few:

"Am I really what I know I can be?"

"Have I set up a program for myself of where I would like to be a year from now, two years from now, or even five years from now?"

"Can a POSITIVE ATTITUDE do all it says it can do?"

If you answered *No* to the first two questions and a *doubtful* to the last question, then you owe yourself the opportunity to try and develop the third. To your great surprise, you may then want to immediately work on the first and second questions. Once you have achieved a *positive attitude,* you may find very pleasant things happening in your business and personal life!

5. <u>Do</u> <u>I</u> <u>believe</u> <u>that</u> <u>the</u> <u>words</u> <u>POSITIVE</u> <u>ATTITUDE</u> <u>are</u> <u>nothing</u> <u>more</u> <u>than</u> <u>corn?</u>

Maybe you do, because many people do. Or are you perhaps purposely overlooking the power of Positive Attitude because you are hesitant to give this powerful asset the time it properly deserves? Whatever your honest reasons, you are letting yourself down.

In essence, you are hurting yourself. I can assure you that this is the best time in your life to reassess your attitude toward Positive Attitude. Who knows? Perhaps it will put you on the road to success! And isn't this what we all crave?

6. <u>Aren't</u> <u>the</u> <u>words</u> <u>POSITIVE</u> <u>ATTITUDE</u> <u>set</u> <u>aside</u> <u>especially</u> <u>for</u> <u>salespeople?</u>

Not a chance! Maybe this thought came into being because it seems that the exposure of Positive Attitude has been mainly in the realm of sales. But far from it. Many executives, professional people, supervisors, retailers, office people, and so forth, who were unable to develop a Positive Mental Attitude have had their careers seriously inhibited.

7. Isn't POSITIVE ATTITUDE just as trite as "When the going gets tough, the tough get going?" or "Plan your work, work your plan?"

Good question that deserves a good answer. First, there is, in my opinion, no triteness connected with the two phrases. I have seen them in action many, many times and they work. Sure, I'll admit they sound corny as words, but when they are applied, they are significant and meaningful. I believe that corn is a part of all of us.

For example, I believe in the power of phrases such as, *"Enthusiasm is contagious,"* because it really is.

In the course of your business career, I am sure you have seen someone with that magic ingredient of enthusiasm come into a meeting, discussion, or group of people, and suddenly the environment comes alive. It is analogous to turning on a powerful light in a completely dark room. When you apply corny statements to your everyday business career, things happen for you.

8. What is POSITIVE ATTITUDE really all about?

In my opinion, that's the key question that

we must answer to bring POSITIVE ATTITUDE into its true perspective.

At times, I get the feeling that the greatest inhibitant to the concept of Positive Attitude is that it is taken to be, *by itself,* a cure for everything that ever bothered a person in the world of business. For example, the thought might be, "Am I being told that if I develop a POSITIVE ATTITUDE, everything else *automatically* falls into place?" No. That is unrealistic. A Positive Attitude is simply one of the very important tools of an individual who wants to be *the best of the best.* When you add Positive Attitude to the other storehouse of capabilities within you, the results are impressive.

Look at it this way. When you are armed with the strength and dynamics of a positive attitude, you will do better in whatever you undertake. **In times of uncertainty, stress, and self-doubts, a positive attitude will provide an essential security blanket.**

A Positive Attitude is one of the great defenses against the entry of Negativitis into your thinking process and, consequently, your actions. Lack of this defensive mechanism can quickly result in your being engulfed by a negative attitude which, incidentally, can be very powerful in its adverse influence on you.

With the onset of a negative attitude, you

may be forced into a solitary shell of business existence, away from the business world of reality which says, **"Hey, it isn't all a bed of roses, but the aroma of achievement is beautiful!"**

The point is that all of us in the exciting world of business -- from the lowest to the highest levels of accountability and responsibility -- need the dynamics of a Positive Attitude, and I mean even the highest echelon of business! Remember, simply being in a top echelon position does not immunize you against problems. In fact, the higher the authority, the greater the responsibility, and the greater the responsibility, the more magnified become the simplest of management errors.

"WHEN YOU ARE ARMED WITH THE STRENGTH AND DYNAMICS OF A POSITIVE ATTITUDE, YOU WILL DO BETTER IN WHATEVER YOU UNDERTAKE. IN TIMES OF UNCERTAINTY, STRESS, AND SELF-DOUBT, A POSITIVE ATTITUDE WILL PROVIDE AN ESSENTIAL SECURITY BLANKET."

AN ASIDE:

How often have you gone into a store, purchased an item or items and the clerk says, "Will that be **all?**" or "Is that **all?**" Think about it!

I took the time to come to this store to spend some of my hard-earned money and I'm asked if that's **all?** Yes, that's all I'm going to buy and maybe I chose the wrong store in which to be appreciated. Silly? Not at all.

When you analyze that the questions, "Will that be **all?**" or "Is that **all?**" and their *automatic* effect on the buyer, you can see that it really *limits* the customer to *what he or she has purchased.*

Let's look at it from another perspective. By focusing on what you have already purchased, your mind will not think of what you may have forgotten to purchase.

Now, let's try it another way. If the clerk asks, "Will there be **anything else?**", the customer's mind instinctively leans toward thinking about some item that might have been overlooked. As such, the customer is thinking **not of what he or she bought,** but what did he or she **forget** to buy?

As a result of the question phrased in the positive sense, perhaps *one out of fifty* customers **may** have forgotten something and will buy it. **That's a 2% increase in purchases.** Or even if one out of one-hundred customers **may** have forgotten something and purchases it, **that's a 1% increase in purchases** with *no corresponding increase in overhead whatsoever!* Now that's a legitimate freebie!

What made the difference? The positive approach, as opposed to the negative approach. *"Will that be **all?"** or "Is that **all?"** are limiting factors and definitely on the negative side of the ledger.* "Will there be anything else?" *is definitely on the positive side simply because it is an open- ended question. If you're in retailing, you owe it to your business to give it a try. Who knows? You may be very pleasantly surprised by the results. What I am saying is that when an opportunity is afforded to you to try something that is of a positive nature, go for it!* What do you have to lose? **Certainly not customers!**

Motivational seminars that place the emphasis on how to interact with customers are extremely useful and enhance the bottom line.

Seminars should provide an exchange of ideas by participants and include role playing.

"*WILL THAT BE ALL?* OR *IS THAT ALL?* ARE LIMITING FACTORS AND DEFINITELY ON THE NEGATIVE SIDE OF THE LEDGER. *WILL THERE BE ANYTHING ELSE?* IS DEFINITELY ON THE POSITIVE SIDE SIMPLY BECAUSE IT IS AN OPEN-ENDED QUESTION."

WHY MOTIVATION?

Motivation improves self-esteem.

Motivation builds confidence.

Motivation promotes individual achievement.

Motivation emphasizes teamwork.

Motivation encourages individual achievement within a spirit of teamwork.

Motivation increases productivity and output.

Motivation is an inspiration to others.

Motivation enhances the bottom line.

Motivation makes people better than they thought they could be.

When you constantly think of doing the impossible, you have virtually eliminated competition!

THE NEGATIVE SYNDROME

Someday I would like to develop a *Dictionary of Negative Words* which would bring into clear focus the futility of those words -- not only in conversation, writing, or what have you, but also the impact on the minds and the attitudes of people.

Let's try a few: **can't, won't, shouldn't, wouldn't, couldn't.** I use contractions here because I believe that's the way most people talk. It's hard for me to envision somebody coming up to me and saying, "I **cannot** do it!" I'm sure you would be the first to agree that there are a slew of other negative words and phrases such as **never, too hard, impossible, can't be done,** ad infinitum. As I've mentioned before in this book, you may take exception to what I say.

You may think, "I've heard this all before, and as far as I'm concerned, it's all a bunch of rubbish, not worthy of the real world." That's fine, but by reading on, you may just gain a few insights that can change your way of thinking and give you the power to accomplish at a level you may have previously thought to be impossible. In any case, I believe you will agree that *The Negative Syndrome* warrants consideration. *And that's the name of the game!*

In addition to negative words, there are negative phrases. For example, instead of "Did you win?" you hear "You didn't win, did you?" or: "You can't do it, can you?" instead of "Can you do it?" And so forth.

Here's what reality is all about. The next time you talk to somebody, or are within a group, make it a point to listen closely to what is being said. Make mental notes of how often someone will use *negative words or phrases,* such as the above. Look closely at the person using these negative words or phrases, and see if you can discern the person's overall attitude. You may be surprised at what you see and hear!

Try yourself! Make a mental note of how many times **YOU** use negative words and the impact they have not only on you, but on the person or persons listening to you. Being positive in conversation involves mental note-taking and deletion from your vocabulary of those words which may prove to be inhibitants to what you are trying to achieve!

"SOMEDAY I WOULD LIKE TO DEVELOP A *DICTIONARY OF NEGATIVE WORDS AND PHRASES* WHICH WOULD BRING INTO CLEAR FOCUS THE FUTILITY OF THOSE WORDS AND PHRASES -- NOT ONLY IN CONVERSATIONS, WRITING, OR WHAT HAVE YOU, BUT ALSO THE IMPACT ON THE MINDS AND ATTITUDES OF PEOPLE."

I CAN'T DO IT!
HEY, WAIT A MINUTE, MAYBE I CAN!

Now let's get back to "I can't" words. When you have a tendency to use the word, *can't*, which we all do as a matter of course, take into consideration the alternatives to this self-destructive word. Let's talk about those alternatives and see if they make any sense.

I can't do it! All right, you can't do it! Notice what you have said. In essence, you have closed all the options that might have been available to you to actually *do it!*

The next time you are wont to say, I can't do it, just stop and take a minute to think it out.

As mentioned before, alternatives exist. At the top of a sheet of paper, and at your convenence in a quiet setting for thinking, print the words "I CAN'T" in large capital letters.

In the event you are unwilling to do so, then your "I CAN'T" attitude has overcome your ability to do something about it. At this point, you must work hard with yourself, or the "I CAN'T" will become an overpowering negative factor, inhibiting your chances for success.

Come on, at least try! Prove to yourself that

you can. Ready? We'll take it from the top!

On a sheet of paper, and at your convenience in a quiet setting for thinking, print the words **"I CAN'T"** in large capital letters. Then below this title, use a sub-title, **"REASONS I CAN'T."** On a second sheet of paper, title it, **"AN ANALYSIS OF THE REASONS I CAN'T."** Directly below the title, draw a vertical line down the middle of the paper thus making two columns. Title the left column, **"REASONS IN MY FAVOR,"** and in the right column, **"REASONS NOT IN MY FAVOR."** On a third sheet of paper, print in large capital letters, **"ALTERNATIVES TO I CAN'T."** I'm sure you can already see where we're heading.

All right, now write down as many *reasons* as you can as to *why* you can't on the **I CAN'T** piece of paper. It is extremely important that you are *honest with yourself* at this juncture. Overlook no possibility, even the remotest! **Write them down, ALL OF THEM!** Now read them, then re-read them, and then read them again!

When you detect that you have written down **excuses** instead of **reasons,** draw a line through excuses. There's nothing to be gained by trying to substantiate excuses.

Now, get the **reasons** firmly implanted in your mind. Possibly, you may have written down reasons you had not thought about before and which could conceivably be the keys to help unlock your "I CAN'T" syndrome.

Hopefully we're going to turn around as many of those reasons as we can into positives.

Notice that by reading and rereading these reasons, you may have developed a mindset that **you can't,** simply because you strongly believe in your substantiation from the reasons you have enumerated. Now, let's analyze why you can't.

Go to the **AN ANALYSIS OF THE REASONS I CAN'T** page. For example, in the **REASONS I CAN'T,** you might have stated, "I can't because my sales manager has it in for me." At this point, accept the fact that there is probably a reason or reasons that the sales manager looks upon you as he does. Now we all know that his or her reasons *may* or *may not be* substantiated. Only you know for sure. Or do you? Let's explore.

In the **REASONS IN MY FAVOR** column, start listing what you think are the reasons in your favor. For example, the sales manager never liked me from the beginning. Or, the sales manager never gives me credit for anything I have accomplished. Or, the sales manager refuses to accept the fact that I am a member of the team. Or, the sales manager believes that I am doing less than my best.

Great! Now that we have those off our chest, start listing the reasons that might be in *his* or *her favor* in the **REASONS NOT IN MY FAVOR** column. For example, I was late to the sales meeting without calling ahead and saying that I would be late. Or, I failed to call on the prospect lead handed me on Tuesday, and on Friday, was told that another company had secured a large order from that prospect.

In both columns, it is extremely important that you exhaust your mind-stored list of FOR ME and AGAINST ME reasons. And, one of the key elements to secure the greatest benefits possible from what we are doing is to be **honest with yourself.**

Now that you have purged your mind, you're probably feeling better, more relaxed, and much better able to get yourself into the frame of mind which is essential at this point to proceed and hopefully succeed.

Let's take a minute and review what we have done to this point and what we have accomplished:

First, you faced the fact that a problem existed; namely, the mindset that **I can't.**

Second, you set forth reasons you can't, writing down as many as you could think of.

Third, you analyzed the first reason cited, in

the columns entitled **IN MY FAVOR** and **NOT IN MY FAVOR.** What you did, thus far, was to take a logical approach to your problem, as opposed to a shutoff of your mind process, which is signified by the unequivocal **I can't.** In other words, you dug in to find the reasons and then further analyzed them, leading to alternatives that might work. What you accomplished to this point is fairly clear. **You are now in control of your next move(s).**

You're ready for the next crucial step. Taking the sales manager scenario we talked about, let's go to the **ALTERNATIVES TO I CAN'T** page. Before you write anything, remember that you now find yourself in a positive frame of mind because you are going to set a course of action which will benefit you in your endeavors to be successful. If you have been honest with yourself from the beginning - *and that is the key element* - something good will come.

But if one of your failings has been to be untruthful to yourself, who are you kidding? It won't work! That is the qualifying factor that must be placed on the table. Assuming that you have been honest with yourself, let's go on.

In the **IN MY FAVOR** column, you said that the sales manager never liked you. Go to the mirror and look at yourself, and say it to yourself, "He never liked me." How does the person in the mirror respond? Does the mirror say, "That's an **excuse,** not a **reason."** Therefore, I am at fault on that one. Back to the **ALTERNATIVES TO I CAN'T** page.

Write down "He never liked me" and place a colon   after it. Now write "excuse." You're in the driver's seat.

What are you going to do about it? Perhaps you might say, "My attitude was at fault; therefore, I must change my attitude to one of understanding." In essence, **I must change my attitude toward him or her.** "Obviously, I prejudged the person."

You'll be pleasantly surprised if you follow this course, that his attitude toward you will, in all probability, change to the positive. Bear in mind that this factor may be the underpinning to all the other reasons you noted regarding your situation.

On the other hand, perhaps the sales manager **doesn't** like you and the mirror affirms it. Now what? Well, it wouldn't be a bad idea to make a sub-list of the reasons he may not like you.

For example, there is a personality clash or the manager sees you as a threat to his or her position. Perhaps the sales manager perceives you as too young or too old or not a   strong enough salesperson.

What are you going to do about it? Are you going to give up? Are you going to quit your job? Are you going to go above the person's head and report that he or she doesn't like you? Are you going to spread nasty rumors about that person?

Obviously, none of the above choices present a viable answer. *And remember, it need not be a sales manager.* That's only an example. It could just as well be a co-worker, foreman, supervisor, manager, middle manager, top executive.

The important thing to remember here is that regardless of the position or level of accountability and responsibility, we are all human beings, subject to many of the same emotions, uncertainties, vulnerabilities, and a desire to achieve.

The real choice is that unless we do something about our situation, we will continue working with that individual in a somewhat hostile environment. The challenge is basic in nature.

We are unable to motivate ourselves when there is a negative situation that stands in our path toward success and we take no action to resolve it!

Now back to our scenario. The Sales Manager doesn't like us. Let's think it out.

1. There must be a *reason or reasons* that the Sales Manager doesn't like us.

2. It is our responsibility to think about our business association with him or her and try to determine if there is anything we might have inadvertently done - that triggered this negative response. As we determined before, we can think of none. Fine. Then the Sales Manager doesn't like us because of *his or her* reasons, not ours!

3. Now, the answer to our problem can be simple or as complex as we choose to make it. Personally, I have always been a firm believer that *simple is better!* Thinking in a complex manner breeds complex thoughts, and complex thoughts oftentimes cloud the *real* issues.

4. Are there answers? I believe there is a concise powerful approach to this situation. The reason I feel this way is because it draws upon the individual's empathy, without a *confrontation or a mentally combative environment,* wrapped up in one simple question. Of course, it is important that it be asked at an opportune

time, when the Sales Manager is not rushed or tensed by the day's situations and involvements.

5. The question: "Did I let you down or fail you in any way?"

6. Look in the mirror and say it to the reflection that you pretend is your Sales Manager. Say it at least two times. If you were he or she, how would you respond? Be sincere when you ask the question, inject an honest smile, and look that individual right in the eye.

7. I've seen this simple question melt even the most hard-nosed individual because it *demands an answer* or could result in a very helpful *question for question.*

8. Here we go! The response may be a "no." In that case, simply respond by saying, "I appreciate knowing that, but I get the feeling you don't approve of me for some reason. And I *detect* that in your day-to-day attitude. Can you please tell me the reason or reasons for your negative attitude toward me?"

KEY: A much needed dialogue is beginning which will hopefully be the springboard to

resolving the problem!

9. The response may be a "YES" in which case he or she will probably tell you the reasons for his or her negative attitude toward you.

KEY: A much needed dialogue is beginning which will hopefully be the springboard to resolving the problem!

10. The response may be A QUESTION FOR A QUESTION. "Why did you ask me that?" In this situation, you simply respond by saying, "I have a feeling you don't approve of me for some reason or reasons unknown to me. If I am doing something that does not meet with your approval, I would like to know about it." The Sales Manager *must respond* to that question, or it may be time to forget it!

KEY: A much needed dialogue is beginning which will hopefully be the springboard to resolving the problem!

11. What happens, however, if the dialogue goes nowhere, regardless of your efforts?

12. In the real world of business, that decision is yours and yours alone!

"He (sales Manager) never gives me credit for anything I have accomplished." Back to the mirror, where you will ask the face looking back at you, "What **have** I accomplished?" Again, honesty to yourself is the key here. Assuming that the answer is that you have indeed accomplished a great deal, and are in a position to verify those accomplishments, this fact is a definite **reason** in your favor. What are we going to do about it?

Think about it this way. Maybe I should have a talk with the Sales Manager. After all, I am going to see him with a NEW attitude, and with a new understanding. Hopefully, he'll be favorably surprised and, therefore, his response factor will probably be positive.

Perhaps in light of my revised attitude, he'll bring up other things that have been bothering him, too, and in this way, with things in balance, I'll be able get about the business of selling. Without a doubt, I'll be more motivated, AND, I will try to improve on what I may have been doing which has failed to contribute to *my own, my family's, and my company's well-being.*

So as you can see, by the simple expedient of admitting to a problem, analyzing the problem, setting forth alternatives, analyzing them, and then determining the best course of action, you may have turned around the "I CAN'T" into something positive, where you **CAN!** At the very least, you really owe yourself the chance to try this Motivational Self-Help System! And think about it. All you needed was your mind, honesty, a pencil, three or more sheets of paper and, of course, a mirror.

I'm sure you will agree that's an extremely modest investment for something that can generate such a high, beneficial return!

I CAN'T
REASONS I CAN'T

AN ANALYSIS OF THE REASONS I CAN'T

Reasons In My Favor	Reasons Not In My Favor

ALTERNATIVES TO I CAN'T

"BY THE SIMPLE EXPEDIENT OF *ADMITTING* TO A PROBLEM, *ANALYZING* THE PROBLEM, SETTING FORTH *ALTERNATIVES, ANALYZING* THEM AND THEN *DETERMINING* THE BEST COURSE OF ACTION, YOU MAY HAVE TURNED AROUND THE *I CAN'T* INTO SOMETHING POSITIVE, WHERE YOU *CAN!* ALL YOU NEEDED WAS YOUR MIND, HONESTY, A PENCIL, THREE OR MORE SHEETS OF PAPER AND, OF COURSE, A MIRROR."

YOU MEAN I CAN BE A PROFESSIONAL?

Who has the right to be termed a **professional?** Is it the doctor, is it the attorney, is it the educator? Is the word **professional** only for those who have received an advanced education? And what about professional athletes? They are called **professionals.**

All right. Let's grant that the above, by virtue of education and training, have earned that title. Now what about the rest of the business world? What should we call ourselves -- the **less-than-professionals?**

I remember giving an hour-and-a-half seminar on motivation to the staff of a rather large restaurant. Included in the mix was the manager of the restaurant, waiters, waitresses, chefs, busboys, and dishwashers. The basic objective of the seminar, as outlined to me by the manager, was to stress individual achievement within the spirit of teamwork.

As you know, to be successful and profitable, a restaurant depends not only on one individual, but on the melding of many human efforts, each intertwined with the other -- each task augmenting the other and depending on the other.

The seminar was very memorable because it made it very clear in my mind that people in the world of business, regardless of their station, are people and are therefore subject to the same emotions of those in any echelon of business or level of management. In essence, we all have common denominators.

I thought about my presentation very carefully. I knew from having presented other seminars that there would be plenty of audience participation, which I encourage. There is so much to be learned from the participants. Never one to stand at a podium, I believe in going into the audience almost immediately, challenging them, asking for their creative thoughts, and then mixing it all together in a feeling of accomplishment.

Moreover, as I thought about it, my mind went back to the word **professional.** Before I go any further, please let me give you my thoughts and feelings related to what constitutes a **professional.**

Is it *what* a person does that constitutes professionalism? I don't think so. In my opinion, every individual has talents and abilities. Unfortunately, in many situations, they are dormant and must be accessed. In others, they are out in the open and the individual attempts to make the best of them.

"He or she is only..." He or she is only a *what?* The word **"only"** is negative and restrictive. In other words, it seems that the implication here is that *could have been much better, but...* Well, maybe so, but we all know that the word **"only"** is demeaning. It relegates itself almost as being synonymous with the words "embarrassment" and "shame." Let's try it another way. **He or she is...** Knocking out the word **"only"** suddenly presents a positive image. He or she is (what the person does). That's reality.

Now we can assume that the person is doing what he or she can do according to his or her talents and abilities - qualified to the extent that these talents and abilities are out in the open and not dormant. The next time you are tempted to say **"He or she is only..."**, you may just want to take a moment and think about what you are about to say.

In the world of business, we know that what separates the top rung from those lower on the ladder is the level of accountability and responsibility. In other words, as accountability and responsibility take a preeminent position, the rewards are greater as well as the status. Does this mean that only those who are at the higher level of accountability and responsibility are those who should be called a **professional?**

Perhaps and perhaps not.

In business life, I believe that anybody on the lower, middle, higher, or top rung of the ladder can earn the designation of **professional**. And I believe that the following constitute, among many others, the criteria which must be met to be accorded the word *professional:*

A. To be good at what you do.

This means to develop proficiency at what you do on a daily basis to serve as a springboard to the next criterion. You are not, at this juncture, in a position to be termed a *professional.*

B. To be better than good at what you do.

This means to develop an even greater proficiency at what you do on a daily basis to help you achieve the next criterion. How do you know that you are better than good? Take a look around. Believe it or not, you'll know it and feel it when it happens! However, at this point, you are not in a position to be termed a *professional.*

C. To be the best at what you do.

This means that you have taken your task and yourself very seriously with that marvelous element of dedication to task and self. You feel your confidence growing. And as you have worked and strived to be the best, look in the mirror... **you achieved!** That's excitement, that's adrenaline flowing through you like rapid waters cascading over a rushing waterfall. Now that you're the best at what you do in your localized area, your self-esteem is excellent, and you feel good about yourself. Commensurate rewards are in order, and in most situations, they have or will come your way. Are you, however, at your peak? Have you yet earned the right to call yourself a **professional?** I'll let you decide within yourself after you have read D., below.

D. To be the best of the best at what you do.

This means that within your group, you are the best, but there's a whole world out there! Knowing your dedication and feelings, you can take yourself one step further, to place yourself in the enviable position of continually striving to be the **best of the best!** This is no different than constantly thinking of doing the impossible. Reaching it will be tough, and perhaps you may not reach the **best of the best** rung, but think about it for a moment! You will have constantly motivated yourself to achieve it!

When you are in this frame of mind, you will find yourself doing better than even *you* thought was possible! That makes it all worthwhile. Now, the question, "Have you yet earned the right to call yourself a **professional?"** *You bet you have!*

Back to the restaurant seminar I mentioned at the beginning of this chapter. Remember that included in the mix of attendees was the manager of the restaurant, waiters, waitresses, chefs, busboys, and dishwashers. The basic objective of the seminar, as outlined to me by the manager, was to stress *individual achievement within the spirit of teamwork.*

As I looked at the attendees, I couldn't help but wonder how many of these individuals fit the word *professional* or thought of themselves as such. I asked myself empathetically, "How do you relate a manager to a dishwasher, a busboy to a waiter, a chef to a manager, a waitress to a manager. *Where did the real difference lie?"*

I believe that the differences were inherent in two words, *responsibility* and *accountability.* The manager had the largest amount of responsibility and accountability because he was responsible for *all sectors* of the restaurant's operation and therefore accountable for *the bottom line.*

The responsibility of the chef was to prepare the food to the customers' satisfaction by using quality ingredients and using his skills to their utmost. The chef was accountable to the manager in the event of any customer dissatisfaction with the food and was also accountable for overseeing sanitary conditions in his (the chef's) work area. And so on. I believe you can see where I'm coming from. Each individual has obligations to perform his or her own *responsibilities and accountabilities.*

It is important to remember the words, *responsibilities* and *accountabilities,* when you're tempted to say, "He or she is **only**. . . " When you *look down* on people, it is difficult for them to *look up* to you!

The seminar was interesting. I covered most of the topics that I relate to motivation, e.g., self-esteem, earned self-esteem, confidence, etc. Remember, I was speaking to a diverse group, yet they were responding accordingly.

I emphasized and reemphasized the importance of each individual performing his or her job to the best of his or her abilities. I talked about how each job performance related and depended upon the performance of *all* team members.

I covered the meaning and importance of interaction, of *individual achievement in a spirit of teamwork.* Each individual on that team depended on the other to guarantee individual as well as team success.

I could sense and see that the attendees were really starting to feel good about themselves and understand the significance of interaction.

Then I brought in the word *professional,* and a lively discussion followed. I talked about the "good, better, best" concept and then discussed the *best of the best* thought as it relates to being called a *professional.* The intensity of the group was marvelous.

Perhaps many had not thought before about the word *professional* and how it might be applied to them when they met certain criteria. I sincerely believe that even the entry of the word *professional* into their thoughts was a motivating factor by itself.

Regardless, towards the end of the seminar, it was obvious to me that the attendees felt good about themselves. They knew it when they looked into the small mirrors I had provided them. My wish was that from now on, a simple look in that mirror would continue the good feeling each was now experiencing!

In fact, when I asked what each person saw in that mirror, one person stood up and said proudly,

"I see a professional!"

I will always remember that person's pride and my own feeling at the time. It is a memory that will be etched in my mind forever!

"IN BUSINESS LIFE, I BELIEVE THAT ANY-BODY ON THE LOWER, MIDDLE, OR TOP RUNG OF THE LADDER CAN EARN THE DESIGNATION OF *PROFESSIONAL*. BUT THERE ARE CRITERIA!"

BEWARE OF THE SELFISH ONES!

There are people in business life who care *only* about themselves and their personal well-being. They are totally immersed in themselves to the point where anybody and everybody (except, perhaps, in their dominated inner circle), presents a threat to them. **The Selfish Ones** know how to take, but lack the ability to give of themselves even in situations where they could conceivably benefit.

Think about it! You have probably known -- or know -- these types of individuals, be it in corporate, entrepreneurial, professional, or other environment. In my humble opinion, these are a few of the many typical characteristics that can be associated with the selfish person. I will attempt to explain how they can have a negative impact on your own positive outlook.

1. Spoiled rotten.

This is the individual who has always had his or her way in life. As such, this person expects others in business life to condescend to his or her every idea or whim, *regardless* whether the idea or whim is good, bad, or indifferent.

This individual has probably been sheltered throughout life, therefore knowing only self and *lacking any regard whatsoever* for anybody but self. This is the type of individual who looks in the mirror to justify that he or she is the greatest - that only he or she counts in this world - and that, in essence, nobody else exists.

2. Temper Tantrums.

Look out for these individuals! Unless they get their way, they spout forth loudly and well within earshot of others. They enjoy embarrassing people in front of others. Objectives of this type are to bring about fear and, by shouting, to hide personal shortcomings.

They believe that the fear they engender will be a threat to the security of the individual addressed and that the individual will become a dominated entity. Two key elements emerge here: *self-centeredness* and *selfishness.* In fact, these factors become very obvious during tirades. **The Temper Tantrums** are threatening to themselves and to your business health.

3. Soft-Spoken Innocent.

Careful with this selfish type! They can be very devious and manipulating. They are the quiet ones who revel in creating problems for others and creating situations that can cause arguments and hard feelings. **Soft-Spoken Innocent** is the pretender that the business world can do without. This type individual revels in initiating negative situations and then sits back and enjoys them. *Don't expect anything, but anything,* from this type.

4. Trust Not.

Refrain from placing your trust in a selfish, spoiled business person. You can be assured that everything you say will be repeated to someone (maybe well-placed), somewhere, at some time. Let's say you're up for a promotion. At some time or other, you might have simply told the selfish person that in the beginning you didn't think much of your superior. Later, however, your superior earned your respect and the feeling was mutual. Now the superior thinks highly enough of you to feel you have earned the promotion.

Forget your promotion! Mr. or Miss or Mrs. Selfish will have told the person who is promoting you all about you, embellishing on what you said negatively about your superior initially. The good part will naturally be left out.

Dangerous? You bet!

The selfish person is the epitome of the classic *tattle-tale*.

5. Moaner - Groaner

This miserable type moans and groans and whines when things don't go his or her way in the business arena. Although empowered to do so, he or she typically takes no action in business situations, leaving this to everybody else. *But*, if something goes wrong, this individual will whine and moan and groan, making it seem he or she had no responsibility in the situation at all.

These people lack class from the word "go."

Make no mistake about it! My point is that when the whiner could have done something about, or prevented, an unfavorable situation, it should have been done instead of waiting for others! These are what I call the back door people because they are rarely up front about attacking and resolving a situation. How sad.

Keep this thought in mind. **When you have a problem, or legitimate complaint, be sure to**

air it to the proper individual. This is not a form of whining. Rather, it is a presentation of facts as you know them which need rectifying or a solution. This is good business for you and everybody else concerned.

When I speak of **Selfishness,** I speak of the *me for me attitude.* However, selfishness of business objectives is a *positive force.* You have worn your halters and will -- utilizing ethics along the way -- strive for your goal. This is a *healthy* selfishness. Along the way, you will have hopefully hurt nobody and will have helped others achieve while you achieved. That is why I constantly speak of **individual achievement within a spirit of teamwork.**

I would imagine that many of *The Selfish Ones* have some connections and may be advanced faster than the rest of us. However, there is a logical limit. For example, let's say that by using connections, *The Selfish Ones* get a prized assignment. O.K. The connection worked. Now what?

You ask yourself, and rightfully so, "How can I hope to compete? I have no contacts. I'm at a dead end." Well, if that's your attitude, you are at a dead end! You have given up on yourself and given in to the *Selfish Ones!*

There's an old saying that "cream rises to the top." Think about it! When a person reaches a particular level through contacts, the business world says, "show me!" This should always be your uppermost thought. If it isn't, your attitude will become negative because your positive thinking process has been derailed.

Take the negativitis and throw it out! In business, the most powerful weapon you possess is a positive attitude -- a *real* positive attitude that comes from hard work, concentration, and a strong desire to be the best of the best! That's what I call *class.*

You will probably lose the battle if you try to engage *The Selfish Ones* on a one-to-one, eyeball-to-eyeball basis. Their own manipulative abilities, using others at will, will keep you from moving toward your goals. Manipulation is their greatest weapon.

In this situation or any other situation within the business world, if you are willing to settle for anything less than the best of the best,

you may hold on temporarily, but in the short or long-term, you will lose.

Now let's make the assumption that you are striving to be the best of the best. In this event, the "show me" factor comes into play which means that your talents are constantly displayed on a day-to-day basis. Be patient. Your talents will be noticed and eventually the rungs up the ladder of success will be yours. Talent usually wins out in most situations, but it may be more than an overnight success story.

I caution you, however, that you must be 195% ready to take immediate advantage of an opportunity when it arises. And the ability to take advantage of an opportunity is to be ready to apply your earned talents and positive mental attitude to their fullest!

By so doing, you will create *healthy connections* based on a positive force of talent, rather than one that is based on waiting for the "who you know" syndrome to take you up that ladder of success.

Whenever you have a tendency to go negative because of the imposition of The *Selfish Ones,* ask yourself this question: Would you bring in a friend or relative to perform a task, even though he or she may not have a *real* talent to get the job done, or would you bring in a professional *with talent,* to do the job quickly, professionally and cost-effectively?

You must place yourself in the position of *being that professional,* ready, willing, and able to meet new challenges head-on. When you work hard to be the best of the best, you'll be pleasantly surprised at the good things that can come your way!

Now you're probably wondering: *The Selfish Ones used their connections, got the prized assignment and did have talent.* Well, in that case, they'll probably stay there -- unless their selfish, manipulative ways begin to touch their peers or superiors negatively, leading to frustration and aggravation. These are things upon which we can only speculate.

Let's take this scenario again. *The Selfish Ones used their connections, got the prized assignment, but failed the talent test.* In my opinion, their stay in that position is short-lived because the realistic world of business, on any level of accountability and responsibility, **demands talent to get a job done, which direct-**

ly affects the bottom line. And that is where *you* come into the picture. You're ready, you have the talent, the opportunity is there, and you go for it!

Although it may not seem like it at times, the business world asks much of all of us. You must face -- in a positive sense -- barriers to your progress in business life and, most of the time, you must make your personal business decisions *alone,* using every tool at your command.

And one of those tools, should be your positive attitude, your integrity, and your fearlessness in **reaching for the stars!** Keep in mind that manipulations and deviousness are negative forks in the road. How often have you seen an arrow go sideways, left and right, down and up, and hit the target? The best way to play the game is to aim *straight at your targets --* **accomplishment and success!**

"YOU MUST BE 195% READY TO TAKE IMMEDIATE ADVANTAGE OF AN OPPORTUNITY WHEN IT ARISES. AND THE ABILITY TO TAKE ADVANTAGE OF AN OPPORTUNITY IS TO BE READY TO APPLY YOUR EARNED TALENTS AND POSITIVE ATTITUDE TO THEIR FULLEST!"

SELF-ESTEEM: WHAT'S IT ALL ABOUT?

Very simply stated, *self-esteem* is defined as *satisfaction with self* or *a good feeling about self.*

As you know, however, *satisfaction* is a relative word and there are obviously many levels of what is satisfying to each individual.

I believe that self-esteem is how a person views himself in his own eyes, almost like looking into a mirror. Let's assume you do look into a mirror. What do you see?

Do you like the person in the mirror?

Are you happy with the person in the mirror?

Are you disappointed with the person in the mirror?

Are you ashamed of the person in the mirror?

Do you wonder what your family sees in that mirror?

Do you wonder what your friends and relatives see in that mirror?

Do you wonder what your company sees in that mirror?

Do you wonder what the business world sees in that mirror?

Would you like to tell the mirror to get lost?

Do you feel sorry for the person in the mirror?

Do you feel empathy for the person in the mirror?

Do you feel embarrassed for the person in the mirror?

Do you feel proud of the person in the mirror?

Silly questions? Not at all. To be honest with yourself, you must look at that reflection in the mirror and answer those questions honestly. That's an important part of self-esteem -- knowing and honestly admitting how you feel about yourself and how others perceive you personally and in the business environment.

There is a logical reason you may find this chapter a bit rambling. What I have tried to do is give you my thoughts on the important topic of self-esteem as thoughts came to me.

My goal in this chapter as in the other chapters of this book is to make you think more than you have ever thought before about motivation. Nobody can supply all the answers, but if you begin to think about the various aspects of motivation, this book has succeeded in achieving its objective.

Back to **self-esteem.**

At whatever rung you may find yourself in the business ladder, I'm sure you will agree that at some time or other, you have heard the phrase, **"He or she has lost his or her self-esteem."** Or **"Wow, is his or her self-esteem down!"** or phrased another way, **"He or she certainly doesn't think much of himself or herself."** Familiar phrases? You bet!

And the fact that these phrases are said should tell us something; namely, a loss of self-esteem by an individual **is discernible.**

In other words, diminishment or loss of

self-esteem can be seen, sensed, and heard. You can *see it* in a dejected face. You can *see it* in a person's inhibited, half-hearted efforts. You can *sense it* when you feel a person's discouragement, the downward look in the eyes, the lips that have lost the desire to smile.

You can *hear it* in the diminution of the voice, the haltering answers, the sudden fear of speaking out.

By all means, do not confuse any of these signs with shyness. A person who is shy today has probably been that way for a long time.

And don't misinterpret discouragement and a downward look in the eyes to be that of a person who is pessimistic. A person who is pessimistic today has probably been that way for a long time.

So what we're looking at, in essence, is the person who doesn't feel good about self, and doesn't feel good about the way that co-workers, customers, managers, etc., feel about him or her – or their perception of him or her. Without a doubt, this person is in a downmode situation.

Always remember this:

Whatever you do that has a downside or negative effect on yourself or others, will – if only momentarily – lower your self-esteem and, therefore, your confidence. Self-esteem and confidence are almost inseparably linked together!

Let's look again into the mirror and give a thought or two about each question you asked yourself. Remember, we are speaking throughout this book of *legitimacy of effort and task.*

Do you like the person in the mirror?

Let's hope you do because, if the opposite is true, you must do some in-depth soul searching and come up with valid reasons - not excuses - as to why you don't like yourself. This is what I call an honest confrontation with yourself.

Are you disappointed with the person in the mirror?

Perhaps you are. If so, maybe it's because you lost confidence at some point and feel bad about it. Or, maybe, somebody said something to you to which you failed to respond effectively. Or, perhaps, your Christmas sale didn't go as planned. Or, the presentation you had worked on so hard did not impress the potential new client. Or any multitude of scenarios which were disappointing to you.

Are you ashamed of the person in the mirror?

If, in your own mind, you determine that you should be ashamed of yourself, so be it. But, the big question is, why? Did you, perhaps, in the daily course of business, perform an act for which you felt ashamed? Or did someone do something to you which shamed you? If so, you wouldn't be the first in the competitive world of business to have experienced this; but, unlike many others, *you're going to do something about it. Right?*

Sometimes, in this business world, we may say something that we should have kept inside. And in saying what we did, we may have inadvertently hurt somebody. Perhaps the statement was made in an emotional situation. Perhaps it was meant to downgrade competition. Perhaps it was said to make someone look bad.

Whatever the reason, it is up to you to determine if an apology is warranted.

Again, refraining from doing it again, or making amends, is in order. After all, your self-esteem within the business world is at stake as well as your reputation.

On the other hand, if someone did something on purpose to shame you, you should talk to that person and determine what caused him or her to do it. You'll feel better about it, and this will contribute to your self-esteem.

Do you wonder what your family sees in that mirror?

You're in the best position to provide that answer.

Do you wonder what your friends and relatives see in that mirror?

You're in the best position to provide that answer.

Do you wonder what your company sees in that mirror?

In all probability, your company would like to see an individual (yourself) in that mirror who has a well-established self-esteem, a person who is disciplined, a person with a lot of confidence, **a person who has a strong, unerring belief in self, family, and company.**

And your company wants to see reflected a person who can contribute to your well-being and your family's well-being while contributing to the well-being of your company. Each of these desires are tied in to the personal as well as company bottom lines.

Do you wonder what the business world sees in that mirror?

The business arena is tough, demanding, and typically unyielding. The business arena looks for results -- the bottom line. And to achieve these results, the business arena looks to those individuals who have or are capable of developing a high level of talent within their given tasks, regardless of the rung on the ladder.

The business arena looks for individuals with a strong sense of self-esteem and resultant strong confidence level. The business arena sees you in that mirror as a person with **potential** to be the **best of the best.** The business arena can see no further than the person in the mirror; but **you can, because only you can work toward making the best of that potential!**

Would you like to tell that mirror to get lost?

If you would, you obviously dislike what you see. Now the big question is *why?* I believe the very essence of raising self-esteem is to be **honest with yourself and tell it like it really is with no holds barred.** Think about it! How can you possibly begin to improve something if you fail to admit that something is wrong? It simply will not work. Sure, you can deceive yourself, but this is **yourself,** so why would you want to kid **yourself?** For you, **yourself** is what your life is all about!

But once you admit that something is wrong and something should be done about it, you will feel a powerful sense of relief. Suddenly, from that sense of frustration with yourself, you will have crossed over into the world of positive motivation. In all probability you will feel an enhanced self-esteem because you *admitted to a problem* and are going to do something about it. Nobody says it is easy to admit to a problem, but doing so opens up new, positive possibilities for you.

Once you have admitted to a problem, you are on the threshold of working hard to resolve that problem. **Goodby negativitis, and welcome to positivitis!**

Do you feel sorry for that person in the mirror?

Look out. Danger signs. At times, I guess, each of us feels sorry for ourselves, and this could be attributable to human nature. Maybe we failed to make that big sale. Maybe we didn't get that big promotion we thought was in the bag. Maybe our presentation to the Board of Directors didn't go the way we had envisioned. Maybe our product flow wasn't up to snuff. Maybe our retail line failed to go as well as we thought it would. And maybe, maybe, maybe.

Now what? Well, we have two very important choices here. We can go negative and stay at that level. In this instance, it appears to me that what will set in is **self-pity.**

Now this is a serious situation because it will be difficult to come out of it. Self-pity serves no other purpose than to dig you further into the depths of negativitis.

Reason it out! Others in the business world have probably faced the same situation you are facing now. Did they go into a self-pity mode? Did they give up, left to languishing about their dire straits? I'll bet that if you had a chance to talk to many successful people, you would learn that they faced the same situation. But I'll bet you would also discover that it was **how** they handled the situation that made them winners!

The successful person puts first things first, and that is to be **honest with self.** I believe that's very important. These individuals also faced the same two choices, but once having determined and analyzed the problem, they discounted the choice of self-pity and chose another alternative.

They chose to go **positive** in their thinking. In other words, they were *honest with themselves.* As such, they were able to learn from themselves what the real problems were. Once having done so, they were able to take appropriate steps to move *upward* in their battle to build self-esteem. Their positive choice makes the most sense.

When you place the gear of your mind in reverse, that's where you'll go. But reverse is hard work. Take an automobile, for example. How far can you go in reverse? First of all, it's against the law to drive on a street in reverse!

Since that's the case, shouldn't it be against your own law to put your self-esteem in reverse? More than that.

A car is difficult to control in reverse gear. And, you're constantly straining your neck to keep the car in a semblance of direction.

Now you think I'm being silly because who would ever drive down the street in reverse? And that's exactly what I'm saying when it comes down to your self-esteem. Why would you want to drive in reverse, when pure logic tells us that to move **forward,** we put our gear in drive (forward) position.

Do you see what's happening? Driving an automobile forward is not against the law. It is keeping in the mainstream of traffic. It does not strain your neck. In fact, we find ourselves in a relaxed frame of mind, a mind which is then capable of thinking correctly and **positively!**

So when you start feeling sorry for yourself, search hard for the negative reasons, analyze them, and try to do something about them. Refuse, under any circumstances, to open the door to self-pity. Once in, it's possible that self-pity will **lock itself in.**

Do you feel empathy for the person in the mirror?

In a sense, can you identify with that person in the mirror? Empathy is to be able to place yourself in somebody else's frame of mind to try to understand what makes him or her tick and to respond with that feeling in mind. But here, we're talking about *ourself.*

Therefore, we are not trying to place ourselves in somebody else's mind. We are simply looking at ourself in the mirror and empathizing. But we are identifying with ourself to the point that we have been honest with ourself and have listened to our story. At that point, our empathy for ourself should make any negative situation we feel for ourselves of a very temporary nature, and we should place plans in action to overcome it quickly. Then -- and only then -- will we find our self-esteem increasing.

Do you feel embarrassed for the person in the mirror?

I firmly believe that embarrassment of ourselves comes when we have failed to achieve to the level of our capabilities. However, our embarrassment also comes from what we do. For example, we may perceive ourselves as **I'm only a...** There it comes again, that lowering of self-esteem. But as stated before in this book, it's not what you do (assuming all levels of legitimacy are in order), but *how well you do it!*

One of my memorable experiences was when I gave a motivational seminar to a group of pest control technicians and salespeople. Many of them felt, "Well, I'm **only** a bug killer!" This thinking, of course, was a constant drag on their self-esteem. They related instances of being at parties where people would talk about their jobs, what they had accomplished, and how great they felt about it!

Right then and there, something very important struck me which has remained with me throughout these years. A way for the *bug killers* to establish **their credibility** was to talk to the others at the party about *what* they did, *how* they did it, and *how well* they did it. For example, how often have you wondered about the habits of mice and roaches and bees and wasps? Most people do, I reasoned, because fear of pests (insects, rodents, etc.), is a major fear among our populace.

So I took the chance and told them that at the next party or when in a group, they should describe to people what mice and rats are about and tell it with pride. For example, mice are unique creatures and can squeeze through a hole the size of a dime. Mice can jump from eight feet to a floor without injury. They can survive in a cold storage facility at fourteen-degrees fahrenheit. Rats can squeeze through a hole the size of a quarter. They can also gnaw through hard substances such as bone and aluminum. And, rats are excellent swimmers.

The suggestion was met with enthusiasm because as a discussion group that day we had made an important breakthrough. Pure reasoning told me that the more they talked about what they did, the greater would be their pride and a greater level of self-esteem would be engendered. Plus, they would take a greater interest in what they did, would experience improved performance, feel better about themselves, be self-motivated, and very importantly, forget about being *"bug killers"* and become **pest control professionals.**

Of course, this assumes that they were following the criteria to be called a professional, which was discussed earlier in this book.

One more incident -- with the same company -- comes to mind.

As the marketing/management consultant to this company, I worked closely with the president and the chairman of the board -- both of whom I sincerely respected. In most instances, I worked with the president. Our ideas on marketing, management, and motivation were almost identical.

At that time, a young man applied for a position as a salesperson. The president had previously advised me that he would like to build up his sales force and later select one salesperson who had exemplified self-motivation, exceptional sales skills as well as leadership, to be sales manager. The assignment at that point would be to build up the sales staff.

Back to the young man.

We talked to this young man. His sincere enthusiasm bowled us over; but more than that, we were amazed at his confidence. One of his conditions for employment was that if he met a prescribed sales goal within his first year, the company would give him a luxury automobile to serve as his company car. Whew!

His sales the first year were outstanding, and he did acquire his luxury car. But serious problems persisted. Notwithstanding his sales success, he had a low self-esteem about the type of work he did; namely, pest control. He saw himself as *only a "bug killer."*

The president and I went to work in a separate series of discussions with him. We pointed out that *without pest control,* America would capitulate to pests, our sanitation facilities would be in shambles, disease would become rampant, our food and food supply systems would be contaminated, and our work and home environments would be saturated with unwelcome pests.

I am happy to say that did it! He had not thought of the overall contributions of pest control to the well-being of society; but now, armed with these facts about pest control, his self-esteem turned around 100 percent to the positive side of the self-esteem ledger. He did become sales manager and eventually built up a powerful sales force.

And most important of all, he was motivated to instill the same sense of self-esteem in every one of his salespeople.

There is an important insight that one can gain from this experience. In his case, he may have possessed all the confidence in his sales abilities -- and he proved it, yet in *what* he did, his self-esteem was at a dangerously low level. By looking in the mirror, and being **honest** with himself, he recognized the problem, and **did something about it!**

Corny? Perhaps. But, as I said before, life itself is corny.

Do you feel proud of the person in the mirror?

When you feel **honestly and sincerely** proud of that person in the mirror, I tip my hat to you. Just as we were asked to be honest with ourselves when we questioned ourselves about low levels of self-esteem, we should be honest with ourselves and ask *why we feel good about ourselves.* Careful here. The last thing we want to do is deceive ourselves by saying we are proud, when there is really nothing, in reality, to support this stance.

Keep in mind that it's a motivationally-sound idea to determine *why* you're proud. For example, you started your own enterprise   and it's doing well, or you got that coveted promotion, or your holiday sales broke all records, or your top management meeting ironed out some difficult problems and set up positive challenges for the future, or you were made an assistant to an executive, or you became executive secretary, or you were made manager of computer operations, ad infinitum.

Feels great, doesn't it? See what happened? By your very **accomplishments,** your self-esteem - with no prodding - **automatically** went up. As it went up, you felt good about yourself. Simultaneoulsy, your confidence level increased, and probably you set your goals higher than ever before. **Note the importance of accomplishment toward your confidence level.**

As stated earlier in this book, it is critical for you to realize that as you progress and strive and drive hard for even greater successes, there is a distinct possibility that along the way you will lose confidence temporarily. That's healthy because it forces you to re-evaluate yourself and your goals, and you will make changes accordingly. The key thing is that you accept the loss of confidence and block out negativitis.

And it bears repeating at this time. **You can only lose confidence if you had it in the first place. You have no confidence to lose if you never had it!**

"WHATEVER YOU DO THAT HAS A DOWNSIDE OR NEGATIVE EFFECT ON YOURSELF OR OTHERS WILL LOWER YOUR SELF-ESTEEM AND, THEREFORE, YOUR CONFIDENCE LEVEL. SELF-ESTEEM AND CONFIDENCE ARE ALMOST INSEPARABLY LINKED TOGETHER!"

THE CONCEPT OF *EARNED* SELF-ESTEEM

In my opinion, and from what I have seen in action throughout the years, the best self-esteem is the **earned** self-esteem.

Now you may rightfully wonder, what the heck is **earned** self-esteem? Well, **earned** self-esteem is simply the cumulative of small achievements. Let me explain.

We all know that a ladder has a number of rungs. We also know that to get to the top of the ladder - unless we have learned to fly - we typically go up a rung at a time. Sure, if we happen to have extra long legs, we may take the rungs two at a time. Fine.

But we all realize that to reach the top, we have to start somewhere, be it the first rung or because of education or experience or expertise, the second or third rung. I think you will agree that we **must all start somewhere!**

Let's put everything into perspective. When we were children, our parents had given us a piggy bank. The piggy bank was a symbol of what could be accomplished by saving a little every day. We might not count how many pennies, nickels, and quarters we deposited into it every day, but if a week went by and we counted, we would be pleasantly surprised how the amount had increased!

I believe that business life is no different.

Our careers, business enterprises, and professions are no different than the *piggy bank*. What we put into it in terms of effort and hard work will surprise us with its rewards.

And every positive surprise will be welcome, make us feel better, and increase our self-esteem. Too simplistic? Not on your life, because the essence of understanding even the most complex situations is to bring the components and parts into their simplest form. *That's how we communicate and understand each other in this complex business world!*

I have often been amazed in talking to a large variety of individuals in the business arena that the attainment of money is secondary to recognition by peers. When I thought about it at length, it hit me like a blockbuster; **these individuals had set their sights on particular goals and objectives and had haltered themselves to reach those goals.**

But the key element was that they accepted the thesis that it would be done rung by rung (hopefully skipping a few along the way) and plateau by plateau. What they craved was **recognition** of their skills and talents and the achievements that they brought forth in a highly-competitive business environment.

At this point, they were not concerned about money!

I thought about that at length, too. I realized the basic reason they were unconcerned about money was that **by recognition of their peers and those in higher levels, money would come almost automatically because of that recognition.**

I think there's a lesson to be learned here.
Each and every one of us has some kind of talent which can provide a benefit to business. When I say this, remember that it's not **what** you do (legitimacy), but **how well you do it.**

So forget the idea of becoming a millionaire overnight. Forget the idea that there is some get-rich-quick concept especially designed for you. Rather, think reality -- the reality that dictates that success and achievements do not come automatically.

For example, a child does not suddenly get up and walk at the age of three months. It takes time and effort for that child to even *try* to stand and then fall back into the sitting position. But the goal of walking doesn't waver.

Day by day, week by week, month by month, the child's strength increases, and the falls become less frequent. Suddenly, one day, there's that child **walking!** The cumulative effect of all those efforts has been rewarded with achievement.

Earned self-esteem is no different. We take it a step at a time, a rung at a time. Every plateau we reach -- regardless how small -- is an achievement in our forward progress and bolsters our self-esteem and confidence. Now we are ready for the next step, the next rung, and the next plateau. Little by little, our growing confidence challenges us to greater achievements. With our **growing self-esteem** as the basic foundation, we are building that fifty-story building, floor by floor.

What do we need to enter the **earned** self-esteem environment? Here are a few thoughts and ideas that may be beneficial to you.

We need to look into the future in the light of today.

We need to be honest with ourselves regarding our basic talents and abilities.

We need to be realistic about our weaknesses and how they affect us.

We need to make the adrenaline flow as we contemplate today and tomorrow and generate

excitement in self.

We need to take upon ourselves at least an initial bit of self-esteem.

We need to recognize that the road to success in the business world is at times rocky.

We need to generate an initial sense of confidence to give us the necessary impetus.

Let's look at a thought or two about the above.

We need to look into the future in the light of today.

In essence, what we are doing is hoping to be at some level at some point down the line. If we fail to set even the most miniscule goals, how can we get there? For example, as you look down the line in your current job, what will it take to be more successful? Maybe it's to earn more experience or more expertise; or, perhaps it will take additional education which might be accomplished in night school while retaining your job.

Perhaps it might mean looking for another

job which might offer you a greater opportunity to work toward the achievement of goals you have set. Whatever it is, looking into the future **today** will be an immeasurable asset to you in the long run. As you progress, you will want to continually monitor, reassess your objectives, and realistically analyze the possibilities. This will motivate you to even greater successes!

We need to be realistic about our weaknesses and how they affect us.

For example, as we started to climb the first rung of the ladder, we were realistic about which field of business we wanted to enter. As a non-mechanical person, I certainly would have stayed away from any type of task which required mechanical expertise. Neither would I have attempted to become a plumber or carpenter.

I would have refrained from these endeavors because I am weak in them and, in an honest appraisal of myself, recognized the fact. By the process of elimination, I looked for what suited me best. Now there are many people who are naturally talented mechanically. For them, the pursuit of experience and training in their particular niche will definitely help stimulate self-esteem by building on what comes almost naturally.

Another example: many individuals are creative by nature or have artistic talents. Recognition of the fields into which they fit and the opportunities available are important. Each of us cannot do everything, but it is important to realize that **we all have a niche to fill** and finding it is primary to our success.

So, recognizing what we are unable to do will motivate us toward the discovery of what we are best adapted for, and go for it!

A caveat. In many instances, you may not find something that is in your area of interest or expertise. In this situation, you may be obliged to take on a job simply for the purpose of paying your bills and biding your time until something in your field does come along.

Or, you may find that this job is interesting and you may adapt to it and go up the ladder there. You never know. But what you should know, is that *honest motivation* will help you get where you want to go.

We need to make the adrenaline flow as

we contemplate today and tomorrow and generate excitement in ourselves.

Simply stated, we are talking here about that magic ingredient of *real* enthusiasm that comes from a belief in self and all the good things that come from it. We are talking about a look into the future and what it holds for us if we are willing to **earn** the dreams we have set. Without that enthusiasm, the adrenaline will not flow, and our self-esteem will not go up, and the confidence we need will fail to develop.

We need to be honest with ourselves regarding our basic talents and abilities.

Assuming we are looking for a promotion, but have not yet developed the talents that will **earn** that promotion, we really have no right to expect it. The key question that now poses itself is: **what can we do to earn that promotion?** It is up to us to assess the situation and see what has to be done. For example, it may be to refine our skills or augment our knowledge within our field. Understanding what it will take to reach our goals is paramount to reaching them.

Along the way, we must be honest with ourselves and those to whom we are accountable in our analysis of our own talents and abilities. "Biting off more than we can chew" can work to our disadvantage. However, this is not to say that we should refrain from reaching for the stars in developing our talents and abilities.

We need to take upon ourselves at least an initial bit of self-esteem.

This is a factor without which little will work. We must convince ourselves we belong in the world of business, that we definitely have something to offer, and that we will not let ourselves down or anybody else down with whom we are associated or will be associated in the future. It is this understanding of ourselves that will eventually make us **winners.**

"EACH OF US CANNOT DO EVERYTHING, BUT IT IS IMPORTANT TO REALIZE THAT *WE ALL HAVE A NICHE TO FILL* AND FINDING IT IS PRIMARY TO OUR SUCCESS."

A MESSAGE OF THANKS—

During a particularly stressful period for me (my father was very ill), our company had embarked on an intensive schedule of nation-wide convention participation.

At that time, it was my responsibility to coordinate all the various elements: sales personnel, technical personnel, displays, product, housing, transportation, ad infinitum.

With the assistance of many understanding co-workers and their gladly-given second efforts, the show went off flawlessly.

I made sure to personally thank each of the individuals involved. Unfortunately, my father passed away and I was off from work several days.

When I returned to work, there was an envelope on my desk from the sales manager, and in it, a letter. The words were simple, the message was short. In essence, it said, *"thanks... your efforts in your time of crisis and the efforts expended by all personnel involved were above and beyond the call of duty and are sincerely appreciated."*

I was deeply touched by the memo. *It motivated me; it inspired me.* It made me **feel good about myself** when I looked in the mirror. As long as I live, the thought of that kindness shown to me will always serve to re-motivate me -- to charge my batteries. *And it cost my company nothing!*

Of course, at that time, I could not have known I would someday write a book. But when the time came it was obvious to me that this act of human compassion should be included, as well as its significant meaning.

The General Sales Manager could just as easily *not* have written the memo. Then what? Nothing! My crew would have felt good about performing under extremely difficult circumstances. *And after all, I was being paid for my work.* But he *chose* to do it. In his mind, he felt he *should* do it! I believe the reason for his success was his unselfish nature and empathy.

As a professional, he *knew* I was getting paid for my work, but his basic instincts said, "Hey, this is out of the ordinary. It *deserves recognition!"*

RECOGNITION!

Another instance comes to mind. At one point in time, I was the producer/announcer of an hour-long radio show. The engineer controlled all the equipment except for the twin turntables and microphone which I operated.

For background music, I had put together a tape comprising fifty instrumental selections.

The idea was to bring up the volume of that music at the time my record finished, to fade it when I spun another record, and to cut out the tape or keep it softly in the background when I was speaking. *These were tough segues.* The first evening we used the tape, there were only a few minor hitches. After the broadcast, I went into the engineer's booth.

I looked at him and smiled.

"You know," I said, "I didn't realize just how good you were until tonight. I just wanted to thank you. I really appreciate it."

He smiled, too, with a look of satisfaction that comes from recognition of effort. It raised his self-esteem to such a pitch that within a period of only two weeks the tape was routine. To put it simply, *he was motivated!*

RECOGNITION!

Sure, we're all getting paid for what we do! However, and I've heard it often, "He or she didn't even say *Thanks!*" One of the great demotivators in the business world is to go unrecognized. Let's face it! People don't expect to be thanked everyday for routine work. That's what they're there to do. But they do have a right to be thanked for:

-A special effort

-An "above and beyond" achievement

-An "I didn't have to do it, but I did it" achievement

-Reaching an objective

-Surpassing a goal

-A strong teamwork accomplishment

-A special act of encouragement to someone who needs it badly

-Helping a fellow employee

-Filling in when someone is incapacitated

-Making a productive suggestion

-And many others that you will think of as you scan your mind

RECOGNITION can increase morale - the *good feeling* that can result in even greater productivity and increased self-esteem. Whether personal or corporate, the end result is an enhanced bottom line!

Too often we take things for granted. And

that's the danger point! By taking things for granted, we have placed ourselves in an almost passive self-situation. We are less than alert about things and events going on around us. When you are in the "take it for granted" mode, you may unfortunately find that others in your work environment see it as *indifference*. And *indifference* fosters a de-motivational element.

Ask yourself *why* you take things for granted and you may find that you are concerned with your own job security and are reticent to give well-deserved praise to somebody who really needs it.

You may think, perhaps, the individual may someday be a threat to your job! What you are failing to realize is that by motivating people on a daily basis, **YOU** will look better to those people to whom you are accountable and they will respond positively. In other words, by motivating others, you are motivating **YOUR-SELF** to do better than you ever thought possible, thereby earning and protecting your position.

"RECOGNITION CAN INCREASE MORALE- THE *GOOD FEELING* THAT CAN RESULT IN EVEN GREATER PRODUCTIVITY AND INCREASED SELF-ESTEEM. WHETHER PERSONAL OR BUSINESS, THE END RESULT IS *AN ENHANCED BOTTOM LINE!*"

LACK AND LOSS...

In the motivational arena, it is important to know that the difference between **lack of confidence** and **loss of confidence** is like night and day. **Loss of confidence** can occur when you are giving your best.

Lack of confidence is usually tied in to a low self-esteem, i.e., a negative image of self. Many times, it becomes visible in an individual's uncertainty toward various situations. Much of this low self-esteem can be related to a variety of situations in the work place.

*The fear of making mistakes

*The fear of being looked down upon in the scale of responsibility and accountability

*The fear of not fitting into a particular work environment

*The fear that your work effort will go unrecognized

*The fear of a lack of communication with others

*The fear of being fired or let go

*The fear of insufficient knowledge to handle work tasks

*The fear of being disliked

*The fear of competition

Let's discuss each one, and as we do, you will discover that what you think applies only to you, applies to many people. You, too, can overcome those fears in your quest for success.

*The fear of making mistakes

What else is new? All of us, at some time or other - probably more than we will admit - have an ongoing fear of making mistakes. It is important to separate "mistakes" from "doing something wrong." And it is equally important to make certain that we are talking about *"honest"* mistakes.

I believe a "mistake" is something that is done inadvertently, without malice, and without wrongful purpose. "Doing something wrong" seems to imply to me that one knew what was right, but may have purposely done what was wrong. You hear people say, "I made a few *mistakes* today." But on the other hand, how often do you hear people say, "I made a few *wrongs* today?"

Keep in mind that the fear of making mistakes is as common as apple pie, but *avoiding* or *learning* from mistakes is an essential ingredient on the road to success. The individual who makes the same mistakes over and over again becomes counter-productive and an inhibitant to his or her company's success. Today, we see more training of the work force, which is in essence mutually beneficial. In addition, mistakes adversely affect a company's bottom line, as well as yours.

Even people who perform routine tasks may occasionally make a mistake. In this situation, however, it is usually due to a lack of concentration more than anything else.

How do you overcome the fear of making mistakes?

The primary factor to recognize is that when you make a mistake, you are not alone. There are others making them, too. The next thing to do is determine *why* you made that mistake and refrain from doing it again. In other words, *learn* from your mistakes. A *small* mistake may easily be overcome, but a *big* mistake can be disastrous to a company's health.

One of the key elements to overcoming fear of mistakes is to *concentrate fully* on what you are doing. You owe this to yourself. I can almost promise you that if you take the above perspective on mistakes seriously, you will develop a **self-confidence** and, hopefully, make the *fewest mistakes, if any,* in the workplace. Making the fewest mistakes motivates you to do even better.

One final point: **because others make mistakes does not mean that it's O.K. for you to make them!**

*The fear of being looked down upon in the scale of responsibility and accountability

You must look in the mirror and ask yourself why you have this particular fear. And you must do it with a rigid adherence to honesty of self.

There's a good possibility that the *you're only* concept enters in. *You're only this, you're only that,* ad nauseum. Here's where your personal discipline and self-esteem come into the picture. **When you believe in what you can do (legitimacy), and you do what you believe,** why should you be looked down upon?

Remember, however, that if you simply try

to **get by** and put little into your work effort, you are letting yourself down.

The best way to overcome this particular fear is to apply all your talents to your tasks and maintain your positive attitude. And by all means, think about this: **performance comes first!** That is the basic foundation that makes you stand out. It is *not* the level of accountability and responsibility that makes the difference; it's how *well* you respond to its needs.

In the business world, you *earn* recognition by performance. People *look up* to superior performance.

As you challenge and overcome your fears, notice how so many things we've talked about before seem to fit in... almost automatically!

*The fear of not fitting into a particular work environment

I believe you would be the first to agree that life is a series of challenges and opportunities. Just as you become accustomed to the placement and operation of controls in your automobile, you become accustomed to your workplace. In fitting into a particular work environment, consider the following:

-Those who came before, fit. I can, too.

-I believe in myself and my capabilities.

-I will listen and learn.

-I will make adjustments and refinements.

-I will work hard to be the best of the best.

-I will constantly keep in mind that team-work is what makes things happen.

-I will be positive and enthusiastic in my work effort.

*The fear that your work effort will go unrecognized

Careful! Your confidence factor is wavering slightly as is your belief in yourself. Recognition comes to those who constantly strive for superior performance! Look in that mirror to assure yourself that challenges are nothing more than opportunities in work clothes and you are capable of meeting them. Then, do it!

*The fear of a lack of communication with others

It is important for us to know exactly what

we fear. Therefore, a simple definition of *communication* is in order. *Communication* is the *exchange* (not one-sided) of thoughts, ideas, and data (information).

I believe very strongly that the person to whom you are speaking *must understand* what you are saying, and vice-versa.

Another key element is to **listen closely and carefully** so that you receive the verbal message as it was intended. I have found that many salespeople are uncomfortable with silence, so they will drone on non-stop, losing the prospect and a possible sale.

When you *do not understand* what the person is telling you, by all means, ask that it be repeated! Nobody feels offended when you ask for a repeat. In fact, in many instances, it is a subliminal motivational factor because it displays your sincere interest in *what* is being said! *Written communications* are no different.

*The fear of being fired or let go

When you think of being fired or let go, aren't you putting the "cart before the horse"? Is there something that is intuitively telling you that you *will* be fired or let go?

Keep this in mind: we all have fears of some kind or other. Some fears are founded, e.g., you will be taking an examination, but you haven't studied. Your *fear of taking the examination* is well-founded. However, if you have studied the subject matter well and *fear taking the examination,* that's probably a healthy "butterflies in the stomach." Hopefully, once you begin the examination, you'll be O.K.

In my own career, whenever I give a speech or mini-seminar, be assured that just before beginning, I have "butterflies in my stomach." I look upon this as being very natural.

Preparation is the key essential -- knowing your topic well and anticipating questions from the audience. If you are *unprepared,* your audience will sense it immediately and react accordingly. Nobody can anticipate the onset of a hoarse throat just a few hours before your speech. But a hoarse throat can be forgiven by an audience. *Lack of preparation cannot!* In this situation, your fear is well-founded.

If you fear that you will be fired or let go and can *honestly* answer "YES" to the following questions, your fear of being fired or let go may be without merit. However, business reality says that people, regardless of their proficiency, are let go when companies are facing hard times. By superior performance, your chances of staying or evading an employee cut are at least enhanced.

1. Do I have a positive attitude to enter the workplace today?

2. Am I giving 100+ effort to my tasks?

3. Am I making strong efforts to learn while I earn?

4. Do I work diligently to continually refine those skills required of me in my responsibilities and accountabilities?

5. Do I follow instructions to the best of my ability?

6. Do I work well with others?

7. Am I constantly thinking of those five words, "The Best Of The Best"?

Remember, it takes only one "NO" to start things going in the wrong direction. So why go wrong when you know what's *right?*

Incidentally, if you answered "YES" to the seven questions, look in the mirror. Your self-esteem is at a high level. You are motivated. Go for it!

*The fear of insufficient knowledge or skills

to handle work tasks.

Look at it this way: you were hired after an interview and perhaps some form of testing. Obviously, *the fact that you were hired* means that the employer had confidence in you to perform your work tasks effectively and productively. If you're an entrepreneur such as a retailer beginning in business, you must feel that you have the skills necessary to operate the business and to look to a favorable bottom line.

*The fear of being disliked

Rationalize at this point. Is there any reason you can think of for being disliked? Has something negative happened in your workplace? Have you imagined something that may not be true in fact? Once you analyze *why* you may be disliked and determine that you can think of *no* reasons, forget it!

When you constantly purge your mind and ask yourself key questions, you are eliminating inhibitants to your advancement in the business world!

On the other hand - and this is very important - if you determine that you *do have* tendencies that could cause co-workers or customers to dislike you, change them!

For example, one possibility is that you have a bad temper. That will definitely turn people off. Or let's say you're always moody. That will turn people off! People have enough challenges to meet on a daily basis without a moody person in their midst.

Another example: you are the type of person who is always negative in your thinking and actions. People dislike that because it provides a stumbling block to team achievement!

Can you take your negatives and change them into positives? Of course you can, by thinking empathetically. In other words, place yourself in the other person's shoes who has to deal with you on a fairly frequent basis. How would you react to a bad temper, a moodiness, a negative attitude?

Not surprisingly, you will probably begin to understand *why* the chances are good that you may be disliked for one of those reasons. And there may be other reasons which you know and must admit to yourself. The empathetical approach is an excellent way to place most things in perspective, i.e., if I were he or she, how would I react? *The answer(s) will very often tell you and motivate you to make changes for the positive!*

*The fear of competition

To overcome the fear of competition in the work place is to *welcome it!*

Competition is the backbone of the business world, both in individual as well as company achievement. The process of working toward being *the best of the best* means that you must continually work toward improvement and refinement of your skills and attitude. Why? Simply stated, others are doing the same thing!

Who does it best determines who will be promoted. Keep in mind that promotions typically mean that increased responsibilities and accountabilities come with them.

Very importantly, you have been *recognized* for achievement that you *earned!* More money? That's almost an automatic by-product!

By performing your work admirably and earning recognition, you were promoted. By being promoted, you earned additional responsibilities and challenges!

Now, your confidence and motivation are even higher, and you are well placed to tackle the new assignments. The cycle which was generated by your positive efforts begins again. At this point, you will work to further refine your skills and work to be the *best of the best* which will elevate you to another plateau!

In our demanding world of business, competition brings out the *best of the best!* It is a continual challenge that provides a constant motivation to be better than we thought we could be!

The factors we have discussed do not purport to be the only situations which are part of a lack of confidence and lack of self-esteem.

They are simply *a few of them!* But once you become accustomed to challenging your basic fears by rationalizing them and then applying liberal doses of empathy, you'll be pleasantly surprised at your attitude change and your increased confidence.

By the way, the key element, as always, is to be **honest with yourself!**

"ALL OF US AT SOME TIME OR OTHER --
PROBABLY MORE THAN WE WILL ADMIT --
HAVE AN ONGOING FEAR OF MAKING
MISTAKES. IT IS IMPORTANT TO SEPARATE
MISTAKES FROM *DOING SOMETHING
WRONG.* AND IT IS EQUALLY IMPORTANT TO
MAKE CERTAIN THAT WE ARE TALKING
ABOUT *HONEST* MISTAKES."

LAUGH ALL THE WAY TO THE BANK?

I have always believed that financial institutions such as banks and savings and loans are excellent examples of the strong need for motivation -- not necessarily because they lack it -- but because their business demands it and depends on it.

When the typical customer walks into a bank or savings and loan, his or her primary business is typically with the teller -- that individual who is on the front line day after day. The reason for the customer being there is usually to cash a check, make a checking or savings deposit, a withdrawal, or perhaps to secure a cashier's check.

The teller is probably the only person with whom the customer may have contact.

Yet behind the teller in the financial institution are a myriad of other services which are provided. To name a few: mortgages, a variety of trust services, lines of credit, equity loans, and so forth.

Why is the teller so important? Simply stated, the teller *is* the financial institution and all it represents on the front line. Think about it! The customer who makes a deposit may also be thinking of purchasing a Certificate of Deposit. However, in today's market-oriented environment, the bank's customer is besieged with different interest rates in a number of print media, e.g., newspapers and magazines.

So from which institution does the bank's customer purchase it?

Maybe the customer will go for the highest rate, *regardless* where the bank is located -- even if it means doing it by mail. On the other hand, the typical customer may want to buy it from the bank or savings and loan with whom he or she transacts business. In today's convenience-driven retailing situation, convenience generally dictates *where* the customer will purchase the C.D.

Back to the teller. What if the customer has had a bad experience with a teller or tellers? Would the customer *want to buy* a C.D. from that financial institution? Probably not! The image of the institution is the image of the tellers!

How often have you walked into a bank or

savings and loan and waited while the tellers seemed to be engaged in private conversations, not even acknowledging that you're there? Yet, they are *probably performing their tasks.* The difference is customer perspective!

How often have you felt that if this bank or savings and loan was not as convenient to get to, you would make a switch? On the other hand, **when the teller treats you promptly and effectively, you feel good about it and enter a positive frame of mind. You feel good about this bank and will continue to patronize it.**

Customer participation in other services which are offered is essential to the maintenance of a healthy bottom line!

How does motivation fit into the picture?
Very simply, it is the key that can influence customers to utilize the **entire** spectrum of services. As you have read elsewhere in this book, motivation fosters **individual achievement in the spirit of teamwork.** When a teller is unaware of just how important he or she is to the entire operation of the bank, that person is haltered in scope. However, when that person is *made aware* of the need for interaction, then things begin to happen.

For example, a two-hour mini-motivational seminar could conceivably serve many purposes. And bear in mind that this can apply to any business that has "front line" people such as tellers who are instrumental in helping to refer customers to other areas of service.

A mini-motivational seminar brings together a group of people who know each other as co-workers. Although they share the tasks, they may not *understand* their importance in the overall perspective of the financial institution. Or they may not understand the importance of their image to the customer in this way: when they perform one transaction or a variety of transactions for a customer, they *represent* the financial institution. They are, at that moment, the bank or savings and loan. When these concepts are understood, everyone benefits.

Let's take it another step. *Unless* the group is brought together and their importance emphasized, the aspect of interaction -- the customer service department, trust department, equity line department -- may fail to be realized. Tellers must be motivated to:

* **Take care of customers promptly and courteously.**

* Wherever possible, take the opportunity to advise the customer of other services offered.

* Realize that their efforts are important to the financial health of the institution.

* Think of everybody, including the president and chairman. Their efforts are interactive with every other individual in the financial institution.

* Constantly think along the lines of being *the best of the best!*

Next question: *"Is it only tellers that might need motivation?"* A resounding *NO!* To be effective, motivation should be extended to *all* levels for individual achievement in a perspective of interaction. There's another reason. The thinking of various service departments throughout the bank or savings and loan may be singular, i.e., individuals in each department may be concerned with their tasks only.

In many instances, they may have no idea of the overall picture; namely, that their success depends on interaction. Many financial institutions or banks are large, and departments are located *in different areas of the institution.*

This factor *emphasizes* the need for motivation! In most instances, motivation that develops interaction is the bond that brings it all together!

I chose financial institutions only because they present a clear view of front-line people in day-to-day contact with customers. Front-line people can serve as an initial/referral point for other services or as the front-line individuals representing their firm.

For example, salespeople, receptionists, executives, customer service specialists, sales clerks, cashiers, and others too numerous to mention.

These individuals, often overlooked and underrated, can be motivated to understand how they *mirror* their company to customers or potential customers. The *reflection* generated has a direct relationship to *the bottom line!*

"THE TELLER *IS* THE FINANCIAL INSTITUTION AND ALL IT REPRESENTS ON THE FRONT LINE!"

"I APOLOGIZE." "FOR WHAT?"

Let's assume you know your talents, personality, temperament, and ability to communicate with people. Therefore, you *know* the niche in the business world which best suits you and which will be your career.

Or do you?

An excellent example that supports this question, *"Or do you?"* takes me back to our Sales Training Sessions at a company with whom I spent a number of years.

We maintained in-house sales training sessions which typically comprised a period of two weeks. There were up to twenty people, new to the world of sales, eager to "learn and earn." Our function was to teach them everything possible about our product, competitive products, overcoming objections, going for the close, and pricing.

In addition, we told them about our corporate marketing support programs which would help them in the field. The sessions were the *non-rostrum* type; in other words, we mingled with the group at all times, eliciting responses to our questions and developing a strong interaction.

I am a strong believer that sleep comes upon a group of participants, not because they ate too much, or were out too late the night before, or are disinterested in what's being presented. The problem is the rostrum. Having attended a number of "sessions" or seminars, I have been astounded that some individuals (the seminar leaders) will stay at the rostrum almost entirely throughout a presentation. Many will read laborious notes. Others will project in a monotone or "sing-song" voice which is analogous to subliminally counting sheep. Let's go back now to our own sales training sessions.

As our sales training sessions proceeded each day, I detected a lack of eye contact, a shying away, and an uncertainty among a few of the participants. What bothered me was that these few were tremendously enthusiastic at the beginning of the class -- excellent eye contact and everything that goes with it!

My first instinct was to take them on the side after class or before class and, through conversation, try to determine if we had let them down or failed them in any way. My second instinct was better. I reasoned: these are young salespeople.

Perhaps they are facing an internal problem or are not getting along with someone in the class. Who knows what the situation might be? If something was going to "come to a head" within them, it probably wouldn't take too long.

My second instinct was correct.

One morning, an hour before class, one of the young salespeople of whom I speak, came into my office. To the best of my recollection, our dialogue was as follows:

"Please sit down," I said. "I've been expecting your visit."

"You have?" exclaimed the salesperson, obviously surprised.

"Yes", I said. "You see, I noticed that something was wrong by your actions or inactions in class -- almost a feeling of discomfort."

"You're right," was his reply. "With each passing day I felt more and more uncertain and more and more ashamed of myself, and the reason I'm here today is to apologize."

"Apologize for what?"

He continued, "Apologize for the fact that I let you down and I let myself down."

"Let me down in what way?" I asked.

"Well, when I first started the class, my confidence was at a peak. My self-esteem, also. I knew without a doubt that sales was my career and I would be a tremendous success at it." The salesperson's excitement while relating these feelings touched me deeply, because it was obvious where he was coming from and the path which his comments would take.

"What happened to change that?" was my

next question.

"Nothing really changed on your part. What changed was me. As the class progressed, I began to realize, although it was the last thing I had ever expected, that I had not really known or understood what a sales career really involved. When you and the others took us through the steps required to be a good sales-person and what selling *really* entailed, compared to what I imagined it would be, it became very obvious that sales was not for me. That's the reason for my apology."

"I can't accept your apology," I commented. "Rather, I'd like to extend my congratulations."

"Congratulations?" The person was obviously startled.

"Yes, because you realized that sales was not for you. More importantly, you had the courage to admit to yourself and to me that your niche in the business world was somewhere else, so you achieved for yourself. I only ask that whatever you do in your business career, give it the same sense of drive and motivation that you displayed during your first days here."

The upshot? That particular individual walked out of my office with a strong air of enthusiasm and a reborn sense of self-esteem.

This scenario happened numerous times during the course of our training sessions.

Conversely, some stayed in the class, when they should have admitted the truth to themselves. They entered the sales field and wasted perhaps a year or two of their business careers. I guess that's O.K., unless that time impacted their self-esteem negatively to a level that became more and more difficult to overcome.

The important factor here is that not all people end up doing what they thought they were best suited for initially. By experimenting, as the salesperson did (believing of course that sales was his field), there was little time lost in pursuing a niche that was more suitable. So even though you *think* you know what's best, it may not *always* turn out to be that way.

It is important to note that I could have motivated those individuals who came in my office to stay with sales for a while. However, I felt that there was nothing to be gained. These young people had not simply *lost confidence in themselves*. **They had made a serious decision that sales was not for them.** I felt an obligation to respect that decision and get them into a motivated, positive attitude to seek and find their niche in the business world.

However, once that niche was *found* and stability set in, it was up to them to continually energize their motivation, enhance and refine their talents and abilities, and then advance to the next plateau.

Motivation and confidence increase dramatically with the achievement of each plateau. You're on your way up the ladder of success!

"NOT ALL PEOPLE END UP DOING WHAT THEY THOUGHT THEY WERE BEST SUITED FOR INITIALLY. HOWEVER, ONCE THE NICHE IS *FOUND* AND STABILITY SETS IN, IT IS UP TO YOU TO CONTINUALLY ENERGIZE YOUR MOTIVATION, ENHANCE YOUR TALENTS AND ABILITIES, AND ADVANCE TO THE NEXT PLATEAU."

THINK BACK FOR A MINUTE —
THEN PUT IT IN DRIVE!

In many conversations with people in a one-on-one setting or in a seminar setting, one of the questions that I hear quite often is, "What can I do when I become discouraged or am feeling down in my work effort?"

Well, as mentioned before, it is natural to feel discouraged at times. It's part of "fighting the battles of the business world."

Some people are surprised at my answer. I think the best thing going for it is that it makes a lot of sense.

When you're feeling down or discouraged in your work, it is logical to assume that your mind will try to determine *why* you feel this way. Let's say, for example, that you lost a sale, or your retail operation failed to get the number of customers expected for your big sale, or the strategic plan you had developed for top management was not approved, or the big advertising presentation failed to secure the account.

The more you think about it, the more discouraged you become. The usual reaction is to turn to the *what if?* factor. *"What if* I had done this or that?" *"What if* we had changed this or that?" *"What if* I had taken a different approach?" The business world is made up of many *what if's*. The key element here is what useful purpose does the *what if* factor serve?

First, the *what if* factor makes us think of what might have been (an achievement).

Second, you are forced to consider the *what if* factor in view of what we actually did. For example, in our advertising presentation, would more light and sound have made a difference? We rationalize and determine it would have made no difference. Fine.

Third, you now go into the other *what if's* of that presentation, and decide that had you done two things differently, you *might have* secured the account. O.K. Write those two things down.

Fourth, what you just did was to access *positive* factors from your analysis to use in future presentations. Stop there!

There is a *caveat* here. Dwelling for too long on the *what if's* can be destructive. Other than the positive factors that can be accessed, what useful benefit does it serve to keep thinking *what if?* All it does is cloud the mind.

What can I do when I become discouraged or am feeling down in my work effort?

THINK BACK FOR A MINUTE –

-to the sales you did achieve!

-to the sales that brought in a large number of customers!

-to the strategic plans that worked!

-to the advertising presentations that secured new accounts!

-to the successes you achieved, whatever your level of accountability and responsibility!

Feeling better? You should be! You have now -- by the simple expedient of thinking back to past **achievements** -- cleared your mind.

Think about it! Armed with the positives you accessed from the *what if?* factor, you have almost *automatically* restored your confidence. Now that you have thought back for a minute, you are in *drive,* the forward gear! What should you expect?

THINK FORWARD FOR A LONG TIME –

-to the sales you **will** achieve!

-to the sales that **will** bring in a large number of customers!

-to the strategic plans that **will** help propel your company to new heights!

-to the advertising presentation that **will** secure new accounts!

-to the success you **will** achieve whatever your level of accountability or responsibility!

And I have a strong feeling that while you're in this positive, motivated mindset, **things will change for the better!**

"IT IS NATURAL AND REALISTIC IN THE WORKPLACE TO FEEL DISCOURAGED AT TIMES. IT'S PART OF *FIGHTING THE BATTLES OF THE BUSINESS WORLD.* WHAT YOU DO ABOUT IT IS WHAT COUNTS!"

DON'T BLAME ME!

For many individuals, that's the name of their own game, titled, "Don't blame me!"

Fine! But where should the blame be placed? On the sun? The moon? The stars? The evening tide? Many times, that's just how ridiculous things can get.

Placing the blame on others, when the blame is squarely on *our shoulders,* is a dangerous game and one which interferes with the motivational process. As I have stated before, **anything that inhibits our motivation inhibits our quest for success.**

The typical "Don't blame me" type operates as follows: "I did my job correctly, so don't blame me." (Outright lie). "Maybe (key word) it was his or her fault!" (Hopefully they'll leave me alone and concentrate on him or her). "Nobody told me how to handle the situation." (outright lie which places burden on person responsible for training).

When you analyze the "don't blame me!" individual, one factor becomes evident immediately: the emphasis is on the *negative concentrations.*

For example, it takes time and effort to determine how to justify placement of blame on somebody else or something else, thereby

relieving you of responsibility. Very importantly, when you look in the mirror, that person
looking back at you *knows* that you were not
truthful with yourself and others. **Was it worth
it?**

Let's face it! You concentrated on trying to
place blame on others, rather than concentrat-
ing on doing your job. **The individual who
perpetually uses the "don't blame me" syndrome as an excuse for non-performance can
hide behind excuses for only so long a period
of time.** Remember that this person thinks that
he or she *fooled* everybody else, which is
probably not the case.

Dependence on the "don't blame me!"
approach is a roadblock to success, because
somebody or something *will be* blamed unjust-
ly.

Look at it this way: if you had simply said,
"Yes, it was my fault," and then explained the
honest *reasons why* it happened, you would in
all probability have been "let off the hook." We
are assuming here that whatever was done or
not done mistakenly is not *dishonest* in its
intent.

Now what? Well, you were honest with
yourself and others, and consequently your
mind is clear to *concentrate* on your responsibilities and accountabilities to the best of your

talents and abilities. Now you are giving motivation a chance to work as you advance to higher plateaus.

It's up to you to work to be the *Best of the Best!* You are in the driver's seat, so the direction is up to you. You know the right road, so take it!

"PLACING THE BLAME ON OTHERS WHEN THE BLAME IS SQUARELY ON *YOUR SHOULDERS* IS A DANGEROUS GAME AND ONE WHICH INTERFERES WITH THE MOTIVATIONAL PROCESS. *REMEMBER,* ANYTHING THAT INHIBITS OUR MOTIVATION INHIBITS OUR QUEST FOR SUCCESS!"

DOES MOTIVATION BEGIN
AT THE TOP LEVEL, LOWER LEVEL,
OR SOMEWHERE IN-BETWEEN?

When we analogize a building with a corporation, retailing establishment, or any type of business operation, we find many striking similarities.

A building with fifty stories is only as good as the foundation upon which it rests.

A company is only as good as the people who form its foundation.

As a building takes shape, each floor of that building is important to help support the next floor.

A company depends on each level, from the lowest level of responsibility to the highest.

A builder cannot decide to build the tenth floor first without the other nine to support it.

A company cannot have a higher level without the support of the lower levels.

A building's durability is the quality of its construction.

A company's durability is the quality of its people.

A building's components, at all levels, keep it solid.

A company's motivation, at all levels, keeps it solid.

Although the above analogies may sound simplistic to you, they are the very essence of the business world. One of the often overlooked factors within a company is the *need for motivation*. The *lack of motivation* can adversely affect the very foundation of an otherwise fine company.

At the beginning of this book, I said that people are motivated differently. How true. On the other hand, it seems to me that there are certain factors that motivate most people to feel good about themselves. Here are a few:

*The pride of learning

*The pride of individual achievement

*The pride of individual achievement in a spirit of teamwork

*The pride of recognition of performance

*The pride of self-development

*The pride of learning

Be it on-the-job training, taking courses paid for or partially paid for by your company, participating on behalf of your company in seminars, or enriching your education on your own, **learning** is a rewarding experience.

Other than on-the-job training, participating in courses is generally a voluntary act which means that you are doing it because you *want to do it!* You have undertaken the *challenge* of furthering your education. Instinctively knowing that education is a step-by-step process, each step reached is motivation to look forward to the next challenge.

By acquiring knowledge, you are stimulated to broaden your horizons and enjoy new perspectives regarding opportunities in the business world. Education will also give you valuable credentials to take advantage of those opportunities.

Learning is a motivating experience!

*The pride of individual achievement

At whatever level of accountability or responsibility, the slightest positive accomplishment should be viewed as a springboard toward another plateau.

The plateau factor is extremely important to understand. **In our business lives, we too often overlook our little accomplishments.** Instead, we are overpowered by the loud blare of media attesting to someones's gigantic accomplishments. As a result, we look upon our achievements as *miniscule,* as not worth noting or appreciating. *That's a serious mistake!*

Our greatest motivation is not always from someone's gigantic accomplishments. Rather, motivation comes as we achieve each step of the way to success, perhaps emulating those who have been extremely successful. One plateau, two plateaus, or three plateau jumps -- it doesn't matter. We're moving in a forward direction toward being the *best of the best!*

Look at it this way. When all factors are taken into consideration, our steps along the way in reaching our goals are just as magnificent and meaningful as the *gigantics!*

Pride of individual achievement is a motivating experience!

*The pride of individual achievement in a spirit of teamwork

This topic is covered in various parts of this book.

Pride of individual achievement in the spirit of teamwork is a motivating experience.

*The pride of recognition of performance

Undoubtedly, for your co-worker, supervisor, middle manager, and top-level management, *recognition* has almost *magical powers.*

In my judgment, *recognition* is one of the most undervalued and underemployed cost-effective motivational tools.

As I've stated elsewhere in this book, *recognition* can increase morale - the *good feeling* that can result in *greater productivity and increased self-esteem.*

Increased self-esteem develops confidence, and confidence develops motivation, and motivation gets the adrenaline going to achieve when achievement might have been thought to be impossible. The greatest inhibitant I know to *giving recognition* is a 100 percent selfish attitude. The "I" (ego) factor blocks out any possibility of giving credit to anybody. People, believe it or not, are not fools. They recognize selfishness and react to it negatively. An unwelcome outgrowth of such a selfish attitude is to demotivate, resulting in a decreased teamwork effort around that individual. Who suffers as a result? *Everybody!*

The key factor for you is to retain your motivation at all times, regardless of this individual. Treat him or her with the same kindness with which you treat others and then go about your business. In all probability, that person will not change; on the other hand, *your responsibilities to yourself, your family, and your company have not changed.* It is your task to continue to strive to be the *best of the best!*

Remember, basic recognition is to remember two words in your career and to use them when warranted. The words cost nothing but, by using them, you will not only feel better, the people who are the recipients of these two words will feel better, too!

Each person in a teamwork situation should be recognized simply because that individual helped to make a team effort successful! In essence, recognition of performance is money in the bank!

The two basic words of recognition?
THANK YOU!

Pride of recognition for performance is a motivating experience!

*The pride of self-development

You feel it and you know it! Nobody has to tell you that you're feeling better about yourself! Slowly, but surely, the building blocks are fitting into place. Each step of the way, you are experiencing surges of confidence. The result? You find yourself increasing your capabilities in the business world. You find your performance getting better and better. And, importantly, you sense the motivation in you and the pride of accomplishment. That's what success is all about!

Pride of self-development is a motivating experience!

*The pride of achieving a new plateau

The above subject is discussed throughout the book.

Pride of achievement of a new plateau is a motivating experience!

*The pride of an earned self-esteem

Think about it! I *earned* it. I *earned* the right to have a high-esteem. Nobody gave it to me on a silver platter. I was *honest* with myself, saw the challenges and opportunities, and took advantage of them, correcting negative situations along the way. By *earning* self-esteem, my performance level is at a high pitch. I have *earned* the respect of people with whom I am associated in my work efforts.

I have built my foundation well and will achieve success, level by level.

The pride of earned self-esteem is a motivating experience!

*The pride of confidence

Confidence in yourself and your abilities is what enables you to handle the tough spots along your career path.

Confidence gives you that look, that gleam in the eye. Confidence motivates you to accept new challenges easily because you are ready for them. Confidence comes from a belief in yourself and what you can accomplish. Confidence, coupled with performance, helps you *earn* the respect of others in your field.

Confidence from knowledge helps you along the way. Confidence helps serve your customers better. Confidence borne of an *earned* self-esteem will take you to heights never before imagined, because each success will be the motivation to even greater successes!

Confidence is a substantiated belief in self without the negative "ego trip." Confidence inspires and motivates you to be better than you thought you could be!

Pride of confidence is a motivating experience!

*Pride of increased responsibilities and accountabilities

The key factor to recognize here is that increased responsibilities and accountabilities generally come from a recognition of excellent performance. It just doesn't happen by itself!

Remember that this is what we constantly strive to achieve, plateau by plateau. A few additional thoughts are critical.

1. Work to achieve! That's a critical factor. In other words, an individual should always work with the next plateau in sight. That should be the objective. What this factor does is *motivate* you every hour of every day to do even better than you thought you could. *That adrenaline keeps flowing and your skills keep improving.*

Whether at the lower level of responsibilities and accountabilities, or the higher levels, your objective should be to continually move up the rungs of the ladder of success!

2. Be ready! If you have been performing your tasks well, you should be in a position to accept new responsibilities and accountabilities when they occur. Let's face it! You never know when that promotion will come along! The most important thing to remember is that once you have been given increased responsibilities and accountabilities, it is up to you to show your talents and abilities to handle the new tasks. And think about it. Now you will be working toward that *new* plateau! That's what makes the world of business so exciting!

The pride of increased responsibilities and accountabilities is a motivating experience!

*The pride of a positive attitude

Although this subject has been mentioned, its importance cannot be overemphasized. A positive attitude toward your niche in the world of business will play a part in your success!

*The pride of liking what you see in the mirror

When you look in the mirror and your self-esteem is high, you'll like what you see. The image of self-esteem is a basis for everything that comes from it -- confidence in yourself, a desire to learn and enhance your knowledge, a will to do better than you thought possible, and a readiness for new responsibilities and ac-countabilities.

The pride of liking what you see in the mirror is a motivating experience!

"IN OUR BUSINESS LIVES, WE TOO OFTEN OVERLOOK OUR *LITTLE ACCOMPLISH-MENTS.* INSTEAD, WE ARE OVERPOWERED BY THE LOUD BLARE OF MEDIA ATTESTING TO SOMEONE'S GIGANTIC ACCOMPLISH-MENTS. AS A RESULT, WE LOOK UPON OUR ACHIEVEMENTS AS *MINISCULE,* AS NOT WORTH NOTING OR APPRECIATING. *THAT'S A SERIOUS MISTAKE!"*

THE LOST ART OF DAYDREAMING...

Daydreaming can be beneficial to self-motivation, but unless you put it in its proper perspective and place, you'll find yourself taking away from your job productivity and other functions you should be performing.

I strongly believe in daydreams. They can help bring you up when you are down. They can trigger a spark of creativity in your mind which otherwise may not have entered there. They can be helpful in setting your goals a little higher, giving you an imagined reach to the end of that proverbial rainbow.

Daydreams come to you in a variety of ways. They may be a tangent from other thoughts. They may just come to you at any time of the day. I would think that they would come to you (at least this is my experience) when you are somewhat relaxed. Or you may just set your mind on a particular subject and suddenly be caught up in it.

I would suppose that everyone has some type of daydreams. For example:

* An executive might envision a decision that he or she makes which casts him or her as a hero in the company and leads to a significant promotion, or

* A middle manager or supervisor comes up with a concept that generates a meaningful revenue increase for the firm, leading to a promotion, or

* An individual in an office, engineering, production, or marketing environment comes up with a suggestion, modification, or original idea which leads to greater sales, opening of new markets, or speeds up procedures and processes, or

* A retailer creates a sales campaign that shatters every previous sales record, or

* The salesperson closes an unbelievably large order that provides big money and accolades.

* Other instances too numerous to mention.

Think about it! All of the above happened during daydreams!

If you occasionally daydream at work, it's understandable because of your intensity to succeed.

The best time to daydream, perhaps, is when you are alone at home, in a relaxed frame of mind. For example, if you start thinking about your job, an associated daydream may motivate you to do better or reach a little higher and make you feel better about yourself.

The key element to remember is that daydreams are fine, but they *are,* in every sense of the word, *just daydreams.*

In your day-to-day business life, *reality* is the most important facet. It is where it's at, where you make things happen, where you take advantage of every opportunity -- not only to be good, better, or best -- but to be the *best of the best!*

And yet, be happy that daydreams are a part of your life. After all, wouldn't it be great to someday reach in **reality** what was only a figment of your imagination -- **the goal that was only a daydream?**

"BE HAPPY THAT DAYDREAMS ARE A PART OF YOUR LIFE. AFTER ALL, WOULDN'T IT BE GREAT TO SOMEDAY REACH IN *REALITY* WHAT WAS ONLY A FIGMENT OF YOUR IMAGINATION -- *THE GOAL THAT WAS ONLY A DAYDREAM?*"

"I JUST ASSUMED..."

Look out! Danger signs all over the place! You make **assumptions** about something or someone that in reality turn out to be less than you thought they would be, or in some instances, just the opposite.

I'm an excellent example because I've been guilty of *assuming* many times.

For example, when I was out in the field selling cash registers, there was a large amount of door-to-door canvassing involved to uncover prospects.

In one situation that comes to mind, I was canvassing door-to-door along a particular stretch of my territory. I noted this one grocery store which had a rundown exterior. I made an on-the-spot assumption that this little grocery store could not possibly be a prospect, so I walked right by it.

When I think back, had I walked in and made a presentation and had been unsuccessful, it would have taken only a few minutes. I would have been at the same spot on the sidewalk where I started. Yet, I passed it by. A serious mistake? You bet! That *little grocer* later remodeled and opened as a full-fledged supermarket with six brand-spanking new cash registers! Certainly not mine. *End of story!*

Had I been more **self-motivated,** the assumption would not have overpowered my judgment. My obligation to myself, my family, and my company *demanded* that I walk into that *little grocery store.* **It was a valuable lesson.**

I can remember others, too, as I'm sure you can. Once when we were going to Florida, my wife asked me to check on auto rentals to secure a car.

I said, "Honey, don't worry; at this time of the year there are plenty of rental cars available." Wrong! After a series of calls, I discovered there were no cars available. Luckily, the next day, I made contact with a private firm that was able to rent us its last car -- *at a premium!*

Had I been properly **self-motivated,** I would have made the call when my wife asked me to get the car and *saved money* in the process. **It was a valuable lesson.**

Another instance. I can remember one gruff proprietor I met in the course of canvassing. I made an instant assumption that he was hard to deal with. Wrong! Behind that gruff exterior was a fine individual who became an excellent customer. Instead of retaining my positive attitude despite the gruffness, I had automatically gone negative. I had taken it for granted that the gruffness was synonymous with a similar-type personality. **It was a valuable lesson.**

"I MADE AN INSTANT ASSUMPTION THAT HE WAS HARD TO DEAL WITH. WRONG! BEHIND THAT GRUFF EXTERIOR WAS A FINE INDIVIDUAL WHO BECAME AN EXCELLENT CUSTOMER!"

A PERSPECTIVE ON LEADERSHIP

Leadership in the business world is many things, legitimacy of task being first.

*Leadership in the business world is the ability to influence others to follow you.

*Leadership in the business world is the ability to stimulate and inspire.

*Leadership in the business world is the ability to set crystal-clear goals and objectives and make them known to the individual/team in a crystal-clear manner.

*Leadership in the business world is the ability to recognize outstanding performance and to reward it appropriately.

*Leadership in the business world is the ability to recognize sub-par performance and to work hard to bring the individual's perform-ance up to your expectations.

*Leadership in the business world is the ability to achieve success, not for the leader necessarily, but for the team.

*Leadership in the business world is the ability to understand that when the team achieves, the leader will receive credit due.

*Leadership in the business world is the ability to remain focused on a goal or objective regardless of the challenges along the way.

*Leadership in the business world is the ability to dream of the impossible while keeping goals and objectives in realistic view.

*Leadership in the business world is the ability to rationalize where there is confusion.

*Leadership in the business world is the ability to be empathetic where empathy is warranted.

*Leadership in the business world is the ability to organize effectively for the best interests of all.

*Leadership in the business world is the ability to set forth plateaus of achievement leading to a goal.

*Leadership in the business world is the ability to strategize when competition is breathing down hard.

*Leadership in the business world is the ability to be flexible enough to meet changing situations and in rallying the team to meet them.

*Leadership in the business world is the ability to maintain and enhance the self-esteem of team members.

*Leadership in the business world is the ability to retain your values, principles, and reputation at all times.

*Leadership in the business world is the ability to reject proposals that would impinge on your own or your team's integrity and well-being.

*Leadership in the business world is the ability to use motivation liberally at all times to make positive things happen.

*Leadership in the business world is the ability to develop and maintain a strong positive attitude among team members.

*Leadership in the business world is the ability to hang tough when necessary and to be firm while being fair.

*Leadership in the business world is the ability to inspire individual achievement in a spirit of teamwork.

*Leadership in the business world is the ability to know each person's talents and abilities and use them to the maximum.

*Leadership in the business world is the ability to respect the fact that every member of the team is working hard to achieve a leadership position some day and to help them along the way.

*Leadership in the business world is the ability to look in the mirror and know that the next rung up the ladder of success is waiting for you.

*Leadership in the business world is the ability to instill a burning desire for superior performance.

I am sure you can come up with many other traits of leadership. If the above thoughts have set you thinking more than ever before about leadership, my goal has been accomplished.

"LEADERSHIP IN THE BUSINESS WORLD IS THE ABILITY TO USE MOTIVATION *LIBERALLY AT ALL TIMES* TO MAKE *POSITIVE THINGS HAPPEN*. LEADERSHIP IS THE ABILITY TO *DEVELOP* AND *MAINTAIN A STRONG POSITIVE ATTITUDE* AMONG TEAM MEMBERS."

THE RETURN ON INVESTMENT

Motivation is an attribute that is not acquired automatically. Were it so, there would be few problems in the business world relating to positive attitude and self-worth.

Motivation in its truest sense comes from within. It is self-discipline at its best. It may or may not be in everybody. That I do not know. But I do know that once harnessed, motivation can be a strong factor toward success.

Motivation comes from an ongoing investment in building self-esteem and self-worth. It develops confidence which, in turn, helps you to do a better job in your business world niche.

Motivation is built on little plateaus of achievement that continually build self-confidence, an important factor in the quest for success.

Motivation is for everybody in this business world of ours, from those with the least accountabilities and responsibilities, to those with the greatest accountabilities and responsibilities. All of us need motivation regardless of our position or task, because the competition is there at all levels.

Motivation unlocks the doors to opportunities through a strong belief in self, augmented by the encouragement of others.

Motivation is an achievement by itself. It is the springboard to achieve where achievement was thought to be impossible.

Motivation brings out the best in you, which is easily recognized and appreciated by others.

Motivation is the reflection of what you are and what you hope to be one year, two years, or perhaps five years down the road.

Motivation is a recognition that the road to success is not an easy road, but the very ownership of motivation can overcome negative situations in a positive manner.

Motivation is a reflection of you - just like looking in the mirror.

Motivation is an opportunity to achieve individually while motivating others in a *true spirit of teamwork.*

Motivation can be yours when you understand its basic, underlying principles.

Motivation requires constant maintenance, no different than an automobile.

Motivation may be your greatest return on investment in the enhancement of your self-worth and self-esteem!

"MOTIVATION MAY BE YOUR GREATEST RETURN ON INVESTMENT IN THE ENHANCEMENT OF YOUR SELF-WORTH AND SELF-ESTEEM."

THE LICORICE STICK CONCEPT

For some reason or other, I always had a fascination for the clarinet. When I entered high school, I immediately went to the band director and told him I wanted to play clarinet. He signed me up and gave me one of those old silver-metal clarinets. My dream was coming true.

But one thing stood in the way of becoming a member of that powerful, 100-piece band. I had to learn to play the clarinet. Proper positioning of my lips on the mouthpiece was an ordeal all by itself. Getting a proper tone was quite an endeavor. Learning the fingering was another story.

Even as a young person at that time, I came to the realization that nobody was *forcing* me to play the clarinet. It was of my own volition, and, therefore, it was up to me. The options were few. I would either learn clarinet and work toward becoming a member of the band, or I would not. As far as I was concerned, there simply wasn't any in-between.

The motivational factors were many. Members of the band wore neat blue uniforms. They marched at football games, gave spring concerts, and entered citywide band competitions. Individual members also competed in citywide solo competitions. Very importantly, to me, the two best clarinetists in the concert band became a part of the school orchestra.

Having weighed all the pros and cons -- as well as anybody at that age can -- I made up my mind to go for it.

To make a long story short, I worked at it and made the concert band, but it was done in plateaus of learning, of practice, practice, practice. Along the way, in that memorable band-room, I met 99 other human beings, the major-ity of whom were just as intent and just as competitive in their desires. Almost everybody wanted to be the best in his or her instrumental section. The better you became, the faster you advanced to the next chair.

At each band rehearsal, I was awestruck by the fact that each of us depended on the other person to make the band sound good. Our clarinet section depended on the trombones, trumpets, baritones, flutes, saxophones, oboes, bassoons, basses, and percussion section to do their jobs effectively.

In turn, they depended on us to do our job well. The *total sound* was what mattered. Obviously then, the harder *each individual* worked to improve his or her technique, the finer would be the *total sound* of the band. And, the individual would be enhancing his or her chances of advancing within the instrumental section. As we moved up a chair, our adrenaline shot up and our motivation was almost automatic -- work hard for that next chair.

The selfish ones, those who were just good enough to make the band, but did not attempt to improve themselves as time went on, would inhibit the band's performance by giving less than their all.

I believe there are many lessons to be learned from the *licorice stick* concept.

First of all, the band is no different in so many respects from sports or companies. The *total sound* of a band or orchestra is the *total performance* of athletics and the *bottom line performance* of companies.

Second, the achievements of each is dependent on *individual performance.* "The whole is only as good as any of its parts" is a truism.

Third, successful performance is based on *individual achievement within a spirit of teamwork.*

Fourth, continued motivation is based on

achievement of plateaus.

Fifth, motivation is based on *recognition of individual achievement* and *recognition of team achievement.*

"THE BAND IS NO DIFFERENT IN SO MANY RESPECTS THAN SPORTS OR COMPANIES. THE *TOTAL SOUND* OF A BAND OR ORCHESTRA IS THE *TOTAL PERFORMANCE* OF ATHLETICS AND THE *BOTTOM LINE PERFORMANCE* OF COMPANIES."

WHEN DOES THE COMPETITION BEGIN AND WHEN DOES THE NEED FOR MOTIVATION END?

Since this book primarily covers the business world, competition begins the first time a person *enters* the business world regardless of the level of accountability or responsibility.

Why the word *competition?* Simply because the individual who performs best among his or her peers will get the recognition and the promotion. But once the recognition and promotion are in place, the competition begins all over again.

Why the word "competition"? Well, it appears that everything in the business world *is* competition. Competition to find the best product or the best service. Competition to find the best-qualified person. Competition to produce the most, sell the most, and be the biggest. **In everything we do in life, we are competing.**

Without the practical application of competition (a desire to be a greater achiever), the world of business would come to a standstill. Products would remain stagnant.

For example, electronic technology would stop in its tracks. There would be no *advanced* electronics technology.

People in the workplace would continue to do their jobs, but that's it. Each individual would be destined to live out his or her life doing what they were doing.

Motivation would be a thing of the past -- a simple memory of what used to be. Self-esteem would be but a straight line on the CRT screen.

Quite an awful scenario, right? But, *fortunately,* that's not the way that business conducts itself. From time immemorial, competition has been *in* and as long as there is a business world, *it will be in!*

Now, you may ask, and rightfully so, what happens when somebody becomes President of a firm or Chief Executive Officer or Chairman of the Board? Are we to assume that at *these junctures* the competition is over and business life has become a complacent "sit back, relax, and worry no more"? I would think that in the the mind of many, these particular individuals are *invincible,* protected by some magic shield from negative internal or external influences.

Nonsense! A look at business journals attests to the fact that the business world is fickle. It can change very quickly because the competition of the bottom line is there, and these changes can often generate disastrous results to the ego and to the individual's accustomed lifestyle.

Perhaps the presidency of a *privately-held firm* offers greater security, yet there is always the bottom line that must be considered. And the same is applicable to the retailer and to those areas known as the professions. Let's talk about that.

Is there competition among the professions? I would think so, or else, e.g., why would some law firms grow larger while others might grow smaller? And why do some lawyers have outstanding successful practices while others just manage to make a go of it? And why do some physicians, dentists, etc., have lucrative practices while others do not? And why are some educators eminently successful while others not as much?

A glimpse into training camps of professional sports teams exemplifies competition well. Some athletes will make it and others will not. **Why?** Let's face it! They are all at a professional level and possess similar skills and are highly motivated. Maybe it is refinement of those skills and experience that make the difference. And in the intense competition to make the team, *desire* is certainly a key essential because this is their livelihood.

It is a given that to have reached the status of *professional* athlete is to have successfully competed and beat out many, many other aspiring professionals. Now, having reached that particular level of success, the professional athlete is in competition with his peers, fighting for a spot on the team, which brings up a few important points:

* Regardless of what level of accountability and responsibility you reach, each step of the way up, you are entering a new arena of competition with your peers!

* Welcome competition! Competition is the very ingredient that challenges us to be better than we thought we could be – to be a winner in what we have chosen to pursue!

* The very essence of motivation is seen in its base form: *motive*. The *motive* is the goal we desire to achieve. Motivation is the vehicle that enables us to reach that goal, that spurs us on in the face of what often appear to be insurmountable obstacles.

When an athlete, for example, reaches professional status or a manager reaches senior management status, does that mean that motivation is a non-essential? No way! As the intensity of competition increases, the need for motivation becomes more intense.

Let's take a look at colleges and universities!

Competition among colleges and universities for student achievers has always been very strong. These educational institutions look for high scores in tests such as the A.C.T. and S.A.T., Grade Point Average in high school, and extracurricular activities in school and in the community.

Competition among students to enter colleges and universities is also very strong. Students quickly realize that there are only so many openings available and the number of applications is large.

If students can be taught early in the educational process that competition is natural and healthy, their chances of performing better are enhanced. If students can be motivated to set goals -- an advanced education, a fulfilling career, or other worthwhile objective -- they will maximize the learning process.

In their quest for educational achievement, *motivation* can make a significant difference! Knowing what the beneficial results of an objective can be, students will work harder than ever before to achieve it! Motivation has no ending. *It is with us throughout our lives.*

When does the competition begin? **Anytime!** And when does the need for motivation end? **Never!**

"WHEN DOES THE COMPETITION BEGIN? *ANYTIME!* AND WHEN DOES THE NEED FOR MOTIVATION END? *NEVER!*"

"DID YOU DO YOUR BEST?"
"I DID MY BEST!"
QUESTION: "WHAT IS MY BEST?"

I have heard the phrase, "I did my best!" many times in my business career. I'm sure you have, too! And I've used it many, many times in my career as I'm sure you have, too.

The phrase "I did my best" or "I tried my best" has always intrigued me. Why? Simply because it is such a *relative* phrase, with so many dimensions of meaning.

For example, "I tried my best" can mean nothing, something, or somewhere in-between. What does this have to do with motivation? Well, stated concisely, if the "I did my best!" was anything less than truthful or is used enough times by an individual, it can serve as a pattern for a passive attitude toward achievement.

If I can get by, simply saying, "I tried my best!" and get away with it, why should I be motivated to try harder? In fact, an interesting fact is that sometimes the phrase is prologued by "Believe me, I..." or "I..., believe me." A qualification such as this almost begs the listener to believe what you have stated.

As in so many situations in the business world, **honesty to self** is the springboard to success. Without it, you're looking in the mirror and trying to kid yourself -- *and others!*

In my own business dealings, I can ask no more of someone who honestly and sincerely tried his or her best. And I can remember many instances when somebody told me *(after having reached a few significant plateaus)*. "I'm trying my best." In this particular moment, my response is basically to the point, "You're not trying, **you're achieving!"**

How do you know if you're really trying your best or simply *thinking* that you're trying your best? Well, let's look at a few possibilities:

*When you said, "I tried my best," did you feel good about yourself or did you feel a little squeamish or guilty?

* If it was an individual effort to accomplish a task, did you -- along the way -- leave certain things undone which *could have been done?*

*If it was a team effort to accomplish a task, did you make your honest contribution *as part* of that team, or were you content to let them go their way alone?

*Did you procrastinate, perhaps saying to yourself, "I'll do it tomorrow," and that *tomorrow* never came?

* Can you honestly look into the mirror, knowing you did less than your best, and be content with yourself?

* If you didn't do your best but said you did, who are you really kidding? Try looking into the mirror and see if there's anybody there except yourself. That's the person to whom you must answer!

* If you didn't do your best and said you did, are you aware that perhaps you *don't care* about quality performance that brings recognition, rewards, and success?

* And so forth.

Remember that failing to take advantage of opportunities in the business world holds you back from success. When you fake out, "I tried my best," the only person you are kidding is yourself. If you do it often enough, your chances for success will be jeopardized!

The individual who says, "I tried my best" and indeed pulled out all stops to do so, reached various plateaus of achievement along the way. If given more time, perhaps this person might have finished the task. Maybe inadequate time had been alloted for completion of the assignment. Perhaps all tools were not available or adequate personnel were unavailable.

Whatever the reasons, the individual gave everything he had. I believe you could ask no more. This type of individual will reach success very quickly because of a *strong desire* to be a winner, an achiever. This type of individual motivates himself or herself every step of the way and accepts and accomplishes greater challenges along the path to success.

When you *really* "try your best" and give it all within your capabilities, you have taken a giant step forward. You have offered no excuses. You have simply done your job.

"WHEN YOU FAKE OUT *"I TRIED BY BEST,"* THE ONLY PERSON YOU'RE KIDDING IS *YOURSELF.* IF YOU DO IT OFTEN ENOUGH, YOUR CHANCES FOR SUCCESS WILL BE JEOPARDIZED!"

AN IMPORTANT CAVEAT
IN THE WORLD OF SUCCESS!

I have heard horror stories from people at various levels of responsibility and accountability in this business world of ours. Perhaps the following could be one scenario: The story of the middle manager (let's call him Dave) who came up with an innovative idea that, if applied, would undoubtedly have generated significant revenues for his company.

Once Dave had tied all the loose ends together, had substantiated his positive-revenue thesis, and had carefully reviewed his presentation to confirm its clarity, he presented his idea to the individual at the next higher level (let's call him Ed).

If Dave had been a student of body language, he would have known very quickly that Ed was impressed.

What Dave *didn't know* was that Ed was *so* impressed with the idea that his first instinct was that Dave presented a threat to his job.

Now what? End of scenario.

If you were Ed and had felt threatened by the excellence of Dave's plan, what would you have done?

- *Would you have placed the plan on the back*

burner to look at it again in maybe two or three weeks?

- Would you have placed Dave's plan in a desk drawer relegating it to history?

- Would you have called in Dave, acknowledged how great the plan was, congratulated him, and with the approval of your next higher level, put the plan into action?

-Although you felt your position threatened, would you, in speaking to your next level, have given Dave complete credit for originating the idea, or would you have attempted to take credit for yourself?

- Would you have felt a responsibility for increasing revenues for your firm?

Let's look at Dave's position:

- If he didn't hear from Ed in a few weeks, what should he do?

- If he built up the courage to ask Ed the status of his plan and was told, at least in two attempts spanning a period of two months, that his plan was under review, what should Dave think?

- Was the lack of positive response from Ed an indication that Dave's creativity had reached a dead end with Ed?

- Did Ed's lack of positive response mean Dave's opportunity to advance within the firm had been stifled?

- If so, should Dave look for a new job? He liked his present job and the security it provided for his family. But wasn't advancement in his work his goal?

- If Dave was indeed dead-ended and the outlet for his creativity was nil, his natural enthusiasm and motivation were seriously at risk.

It appears to me that integrity to self and to company are at risk here. Motivation and continuing achievement are, too. So are the future careers of Ed and Dave.

I believe that Ed's *integrity to himself and his company* dictate that he follow up Dave's plan, get higher-up approval, and put it into effect. As a result, although it is not Ed's plan, Ed will be *recognized for recognizing* Dave's talents and taking positive action for the benefit of the firm.

Is Ed jeopardizing his position? Probably

not. In fact, it may be a stepping stone for Ed, since he is employing talented people, who through their own achievements, enhance Ed's image. When Ed sees things in this light, he is motivated to further motivate those responsible to him. Motivation, such as this, has a marvelous way of filtering down and generating a strong sense of teamwork.

Dave, now having been recognized for his achievement, will work even harder to come up with additional creative suggestions. In turn, Dave is now motivated to motivate the people responsible to him. See what's happening? A synergism has developed for **individual achievement in a spirit of teamwork!** The beneficiaries?

Ed, Dave, and everybody else involved!

"ALTHOUGH IT IS NOT ED'S PLAN, ED WILL BE *RECOGNIZED FOR RECOGNIZING* DAVE'S TALENTS AND TAKING POSITIVE ACTION FOR THE BENEFIT OF THE FIRM."

ARE YOU MOTIVATED TO MOTIVATE? ADDITIONAL THOUGHTS ON LEADERSHIP

As we've seen before, a heightened self-esteem makes us feel good about ourselves. When we feel good about ourselves, our confidence grows. As our confidence grows, our work level and quality of performance increases and our instincts tell us to constantly reach out for new challenges. In this particular mindset, and *often without realizing it,* we are striving to be *the best of the best!*

In many avenues of the business world, and at many levels of accountability and responsibility, I have seen confidence generate outstanding performance. And it is this performance that *earns* recognition and its rewards. One of the rewards is to be placed in a position of **leadership.**

We often hear the phrase, "leadership by example." In other words, we follow the example of our leader (supervisor, foreman, office manager, team leader, middle or top-level executive, etc.) in what he or she does. Leadership by example is an excellent form of business application.

As such, leadership by example motivates the individuals responding to that leader to continually improve their performance. I should point out here that leadership by example requires a *legitimacy* of purpose.

I strongly believe that in addition to, or concurrent with *leadership by example,* there is *leadership through motivation.* Attempting to emulate the leader, of course, provides motivation, but the *old automatic* is insufficient in many situations.

For example, an effective leader sets *goals,* determines *how* to achieve these goals, *who* should be involved in achieving these goals, *when* these goals should be realistically achieved, *why* the achievement of these goals is important, and *what* these goals will produce beneficially.

It is critical that much of the *how, who, when, why,* and *what* of the goals be explained to the participants, which is a motivational essential. The result of this action is that everybody knows what is expected of them, that he or she is an important spoke in the wheel that turns toward success.

Divested of that knowledge, team members can honestly say, "Well, I didn't know," or "I didn't understand," or "Why didn't someone tell me?" Also, work effort may go in different directions, instead of on a singular path to achievement. Another very important factor is that by **understanding** the goals, the individuals involved subconsciously fall into a perspective of interaction.

An effective leader constantly *monitors* the performance of his people (team). I believe it is in the *monitoring* of performance that *motivation* really shows its value. The *lack* of monitoring individual performance can destroy goals very quickly.

For example, by monitoring in the form of daily, weekly, or biweekly reports, the leader will note those individuals who are performing less than, equal to, or greater than expected. For those who are performing less than expected, the leader must determine what the reasons are and take immediate action to rectify the situation for the benefit of the individual, the team, and the firm.

A leader can usually sense negative situations by means of individual attitudes and other signs that say, "Something is wrong here."

Once the leader has spoken with the individual and determined the reasons (not excuses) for sub-par performance and also determines that the individual is *capable* of performance, he or she must motivate that individual to achieve. Easier said than done, perhaps, but the following thoughts offer a few possibilities for the leader to utilize:

*Reemphasize the goals

*Reemphasize the benefits of the goals

*Reemphasize the importance of that individual to the attainment of these goals

*Reemphasize the good feeling of individual achievement

*Reemphasize the importance of individual achievement in a spirit of teamwork

*Reemphasize that you are available to help him or her toward the goals

*Work to enhance the individual's self-esteem and thereby increase the confidence level

*Emphasize "We care about you because you're important to us. We want you to be *the best of the best!"*

AND BY ALL MEANS, AS A LEADER, ASK THE QUESTION THAT SHOULD ALWAYS BE ASKED IN NEGATIVE SITUATIONS: "IS THERE A POSSIBILITY THAT I UNKNOWINGLY LET YOU DOWN IN SOME WAY?"

Asking this question demands an answer. If the answer is an honest NO, then you have fortified yourself that the problem is not with you. In the event you detect a hesitancy from the individual, it behooves you to pursue the issue. If the answer is YES, you're on the way to solving the negative situation.

As a leader, motivation is what he or she wants it to be and with it, a leader can make great things happen!

Does it stop here? No! For example, the individual to whom you spoke begins to perform better. **Tell him or her about it!** Give him or her a pat on the back, or a "nice going" or "I knew you could do it and if you need help, I'm here!" Be sure to take the above actions *only if honestly warranted.*

Dishonest, undeserved praise encourages passive performance, leading in some instances to self-accepted, mediocre standards of performance.

Now what about the person who has achieved from the start? **Tell him or her about it!** Give him or her a pat on the back or a "Nice going, *keep it up!"* or "You're setting a great example" or "Thanks for helping me when I needed it most."

The effective leader generally *knows* what is going on around him or her -- what is going well and what is not going well -- and responds quickly.

In essence, **by example is leadership** and **leadership is by example,** while **leadership is by motivation** and **motivation is by leadership!**

"AN EFFECTIVE LEADER SETS *GOALS,* DETERMINES *HOW* TO ACHIEVE THESE GOALS, *WHEN* THESE GOALS SHOULD BE REALISTICALLY ACHIEVED, *WHY* THE ACHIEVEMENT OF THESE GOALS IS IMPORTANT, AND *WHAT* THESE GOALS WILL PRODUCE BENEFICIALLY."

AN IMPORTANT NOTE:

Before reading the last chapter, it is imperative that you will have read all the preceding chapters.

Before reading the last chapter, it is imperative that you have a strong understanding of the principles of motivation.

Before reading the last chapter, it is imperative that what you will read will be understood in the context of its presentation.

Before reading the last chapter, be sure that you really want to motivate yourself to achieve new heights.

Before reading the last chapter, make certain that you understand there is no magic ingredient that can give you motivation.

Before reading the last chapter, it is imperative that you desire to be successful in the business world.

Before reading the last chapter, be prepared to work hard at what you are told. The key element is to be *self-motivated to do it!* Good Luck!

THE IMPORTANCE OF
THE *I.M.* FACTOR

Motivation for only an instant, an hour, a day, a week, is better than no motivation. *But,* motivation, to be effective to the maximum degree, should be something that is practiced *consistently, at every opportune moment.*

Motivation should be as important to your daily well-being as the healthy maintenance of your heart, your lungs, and your brain. Motivation must become a *part* of you - *to be called upon at any given moment.*

The *continuity* of motivation is a key essential to success. I call it the **I.M.** factor, which is **INSTANT MOTIVATION.**

Throughout this book, you have noted that I repeatedly referred to looking in the mirror. Well, that's part of what **I.M.** is all about. It is important to note that three of the key elements of motivation we have talked about should be kept in mind: *honesty and integrity to self, a strong self-discipline, and legitimacy of task.*

Now, you may wonder, "Why did I pick the mirror concept for **I.M.?"**

Well, it goes back a number of years. An executive, with whom I had the pleasure of working, had been assigned from Europe to head up our USA operation. Given this new chief executive's assignment in America, and knowing *some* English, he instinctively knew that he had *no choice* but to become fluent in the language.

A strongly-motivated individual, he devised a plan to tape little pieces of paper to the mirror in the bathroom. On each piece of paper was a word in his foreign language and the translated word in the English language. So while shaving, or brushing his teeth, or combing his hair -- staring him right in the face -- were those little pieces of paper with those two words on each.

Did it work? You bet it did!

He became fluent in the English language faster than anyone I had ever known, or have known since, and *retained* what he learned. He became a highly-successful executive due in large measure to the fact that he was able, because of the little pieces of paper and strong measures of self-discipline and motivation, to communicate effectively.

I was intrigued by both the power of that mirror and its convenient location. I often wondered how that mirror or any mirror could be applied to motivation.

I thought back to my days as a young salesperson canvassing up and down the street and how I had temporarily lost confidence in myself. I thought about how a mirror seemed to unexpectedly appear in front of me, right there on that street. I remembered looking into that mirror and the repulsion I felt. I was feeling sorry for myself because things weren't going right for me.

Across the street was a man with no legs in a wheelchair saying, **"Good morning, how are you?"** to the patrons of a restaurant.

What right did I have to complain and feel sorry for myself? The mirror then seemingly reappeared and I looked into it. And suddenly there was a surge of confidence within me. That man and that mirror will remain in my memory forever.

Although I told this story at the beginning of this book, it was important to repeat, because **that particular experience was what made this book come alive!**

I thought about the mirror concept in great detail from every perspective I knew. I tested the concept with myself and others in mini-seminar situations, and in most instances, it worked.

I tested the concept in private conversations with people in various levels of accountability and responsibility.

I became convinced. The concept and its practical application work *not once, not twice, not three times, but over and over again, with no limits on their staying power or effectiveness, because motivation is being constantly maintained!*

As contrasted to the executive who used the **bathroom mirror only,** the number of mirrors you can use are many. For example, mirrors at work, at home, in your car, your own personal mirror -- in essence, anywhere you have access to a mirror.

Why do I need the mirror?
You use the mirror to reaffirm your accountability and responsibility to yourself. And to motivate yourself!

Think about it! You are accountable to yourself for:

*Your achievements

*Your disappointments

*Your lack of self-esteem

*Your enhanced self-esteem

*Your earned self-esteem

*Your trying

*Your lack of trying

*Your confidence level

*Your lack of confidence

*Your hopes, your aspirations

*Your business situations

*Ad Infinitum

Let's take it a step further. Yes, you are accountable to yourself, but *there are others to whom you are accountable, e.g., your family. And you are also accountable to the company for whom you work, retailing operation, your own company, profession, co-workers, management, etc. In other words, in whatever work environment you are involved.*

So there you are, your accountabilities:

*Yourself   *Your family   *Your work

Why the mirror? Well, simply stated, because the *only* reflection in that mirror is a reflection of *you,* and nobody else. Therefore, when you look into the mirror, the responsibility is *squarely on your shoulders!* You are responsible to yourself, no passing the buck, no pushing off the accountability on to someone else. You, *and only you,* are responsible to that person in the mirror. How you view yourself is critical, as pointed out elsewhere in this book.

When you get up to go to work, and go into the bathroom, you *look into a mirror* to shave, brush your teeth, comb your hair, or apply cosmetics -- things that men and women do in the morning, afternoon, evening, or midnight, depending on their work schedules. The value of that mirror will now increase significantly!

As a part of that daily bathroom routine, when your face and hair are in place, take a good, long look at that person in the mirror and imagine you are saying the following:

"I believe."

In essence, the mirror looks back (your own reflection) and asks,

"What do you believe?"

And you answer,

"I believe in myself, my family, and my work."

"I believe that today I'm going to go out and do the best job I know how, and I'm going to achieve for myself, my family, and my work."

What happened is that during this short period of only seconds, you have affirmed your commitments and responsibilities for that day and your desire to achieve. *And to whom was this affirmation addressed?* **To yourself, the only person in that mirror!**

When you come home in the evening, regardless how good or bad the day went, you will go to the mirror. The mirror (your reflection) will ask,

"What did you accomplish for yourself, your family, and your work today?"

Hopefully, you have had a good day. Looking in the mirror will automatically remind you of your accomplishments, and you will feel good about yourself. Your self-esteem will go up, as will your confidence level. The next morning, in front of your mirror, you'll be ready to tackle the business world again to do *even better* than you did the day before!

It is imperative to remember that the achievement of even the *smallest plateau* is significant on your road to success! Tell your mirror about it!

Unfortunately, things didn't go well for you that day at work. Tell the person in the mirror *why* you think that things didn't go well. Tell the person in the mirror *how* you expect to make tomorrow a better day **for yourself, your family, and your work.**

By so doing, you have reduced the feelings of frustration that day and hopefully will be ready the next morning to tell that person in the mirror *you are going to achieve this day!*

You will find that when you address the mirror each morning, during the day, and when you come home, it will become a habit. **After a while, simply looking in the mirror will serve as motivation.**

The key element is to do it *every day!*

Remember that motivation is only a tool. It is not the wherewithal to solve your business world challenges. But it is a frame of mind, *a positive frame of mind,* to attempt to resolve these challenges in a positive way.

When you follow the mirror concept and are honest with yourself, you will probably never again look at the mirror the way you did before. You will now view that reflection in the mirror as an *important person* who has something *constructive and positive to contribute to the workplace.*

You will find that when you need that additional bit of adrenaline, the mirror will provide it to you because you will be affirming your confidence in yourself.

This is what I call I.M. – INSTANT MOTIVATION, brought about by the simple expedient of a mirror!

Looking in the mirror before going to work, making a sales call, attending a meeting, or any other task that comes along your way during the day, makes you feel better about yourself and who you are. Remember, you have something important to offer: you and your talents and abilities.

The realistic business world is an exciting world filled with opportunities, achievements, and disappointments.

Properly motivated, you will be able to take advantage of those opportunities.

When you achieve, motivation will help you reach higher goals and objectives.

And, when disappointments and negative situations occur, motivation will help you to face them and bounce back!

And when you need the **I.M.**, it will be there for you, because you made a commitment to it on a *daily basis.*

Remember that one of the important aspects of motivation is to **continually develop increased self-confidence based on an enhanced self-esteem.**

And bear in mind that **every little achievement is significant to your success!**

If you should ever feel like giving up on yourself, take a look at yourself in the mirror and tell that reflection you *will not give up on yourself.* You have *something positive to offer to the workplace!* And supporting that thought to the maximum degree is your own special **I.M. factor, INSTANT MOTIVATION!**

Motivation is a treasure you can keep throughout your lifetime. It is an ongoing investment in yourself that will reap significant dividends for you and help you to achieve when you might have thought achievement impossible.

Motivation has another marvelous quality. In so many instances, we might say, *"I can't afford it!"* But you **can** afford it, because motivation costs **nothing!** Yet, its rewards are great!

And the beneficiaries of your investment in motivation will be **yourself, your family, and your work!**

That is the bottom line!

"MOTIVATION IS A TREASURE YOU CAN KEEP THROUGHOUT YOUR LIFETIME. IT IS AN ONGOING INVESTMENT IN YOURSELF THAT WILL REAP SIGNIFICANT DIVIDENDS FOR YOU AND HELP YOU TO ACHIEVE WHEN YOU MIGHT HAVE THOUGHT ACHIEVEMENT IMPOSSIBLE."

FAX NO: (708) 990-0089

HOW TO ORDER ADDITIONAL BOOKS

☐ Please send additional copies of:
How To Compete With Yourself And Win!

No. of books _____ x $12.95 = $ _____

Add .87 sales tax per book* = $ _____

No. of books x $3.00 S & H = $ _____

Total check or money order: = $ _____

Illinois residents only.

To order by Credit Card,
call toll-free 1-800-247-6553!

Visa-Mastercard-Discover-American Express

Shipping and Handling Charges will be added. If you are an Illinois Resident, Illinois Sales Tax will apply.

☐ Please send additional books with special discounts for corporations and groups!

10 books @ $12.50 each* = $ _____

25 books @ $12.00 each* = $ _____

50 books @ $11.50 each* = $ _____

100 books @ $11.00 each* = $ _____

State sales tax, if applicable* = $ _____

Total check or money order: = $ _____

*Illinois corporations or groups add (.0675) sales tax. Books are shipped C.O.D. for UPS charges only.

Please make check or money order payable to: DINO H. PAVLAKOS & ASSOCIATES
1000 Jorie Blvd., Suite 144, Oak Brook, IL 60521

How To Compete With Yourself And Win!

AUDIO PACKAGE

Whenever you're in your car, at home, taking a walk, jogging, or any time and place that's appropriate, you'll be inspired by this special audio package of two information-filled cassettes!

Each cassette features 30 minutes on each side in conveniently arranged time segments, for a total of 120 minutes of power motivation. There is a special 5-minute introduction that sets the stage for the tapes. Although much of the material is a direct reading from the book in order to maintain the content, the author offers additional insights and new thoughts throughout. Here is your opportunity to harness the power of motivation and generate enhanced self-esteem and confidence!

All segments are recorded by the author, who is a dynamic speaker and professional narrator. As you listen to the tapes you will understand what motivation is all about. When you have finished the tapes, you will be able to motivate yourself in *thirty seconds or less!*

Motivation is a treasure that you can keep throughout your lifetime. It is an ongoing investment in yourself that can reap significant dividends and help you achieve when you might have thought that achievement was impossible. The beneficiaries? **Yourself, your family, and your company!**

That's the *bottom line!*

FAX NO: (708) 990-0089

HOW TO ORDER AUDIO PACKAGES

☐ Please send audio package(s) of:
How To Compete With Yourself And Win!

No. of audio packages _____ x $29.95 = $ _____

Add 2.02 sales tax per audio package* = $ _____

No. of audio packages x $4.50 S & H = $ _____

Total check or money order: = $ _____

*Illinois residents only.

To order by Credit Card,
call toll-free 1-800-247-6553!

Visa-Mastercard-Discover-American Express

Shipping and Handling Charges will be added. If you are an Illinois
Resident, Illinois Sales Tax will apply.

☐ Please send audio package(s) with special
discounts for corporations and groups!

5 audio packages @ 27.95 each* = $ _____

10 audio packages @ 26.95 each* = $ _____

15 audio packages @ 25.95 each* = $ _____

20 audio packages @ 24.95 each* = $ _____

State sales tax, if applicable* = $ _____

Total check or money order: = $ _____

*Illinois corporations or groups add (.0675) sales tax.
Audio Packages are shipped C.O.D. for UPS charges only.

Please make check or money order payable to: DINO H. PAVLAKOS & ASSOCIATES
1000 Jorie Blvd., Suite 144, Oak Brook, IL 60521

MOTIVATIONAL SEMINARS

In person, Pavlakos is a dynamic speaker and outstanding motivator. Not one to stand at a lectern, he goes out into a group and challenges the attendees. The responses generate comments from other attendees and before you know it, there is a powerful interaction between the group. Pavlakos guides and inspires the group, making certain that each aspect of motivation is covered in detail.

"At times, I almost feel that the *attendees* are conducting the seminar. This is the point at which I know the seminar is a success! Participation and excitement are the key elements that must be generated; otherwise, we simply have a speaker, listeners, and in many instances, boredom."

Seminars are available to small as well as large groups. To achieve the greatest benefit, each seminar is customized to your exact needs so that the appropriate topics and challenges can be addressed.

For further information concerning Motivational Seminars or Motivational/Sales Seminars, call or write to:

Dino H. Pavlakos & Associates
1000 Jorie Blvd., Suite 144
Oak Brook, Il 60521
708-990-0772